THE
ANONYMOUS
REVOLUTIONARY

THE
ANONYMOUS
REVOLUTIONARY

A COLLECTION OF COMMUNIST WRITINGS

Max Edwards

Published in 2016 by
Short Books, Unit 316, ScreenWorks
22 Highbury Grove
London N5 2ER

10 9 8 7 6 5 4 3 2 1

The majority of the images in this book are from the author's personal
collection, as featured on the original blog, and every effort has been
made to abide by 'fair use' guidelines. If you are a copyright-holder and
wish to get in touch, please email info@shortbooks.co.uk

A CIP catalogue record for this book is available from
the British Library.

ISBN: 978-1-78072-294-8

Printed and bound in Great Britain by CPI Group (UK) Ltd,
Croydon, CR0 4YY

To the International Proletariat

Contents

FOREWORD

This book contains forty-two writings: a year's worth of blogging. Across that period of time, a lot has changed, such as my opinions and views, but also the way in which I conveyed them. I remember, in the earlier entries, I would tread cautiously when talking of Communism, I'd be quick to disassociate myself from figures like Stalin, and I'd almost apologise for anything that may have sounded too radical. I also remember having no qualms about quoting Republican senator Marco Rubio, something I'd now probably refrain from doing.

Yet my blog is certainly different today. Perhaps it was writing regular posts that provoked this change, or perhaps it was just a result of having read or discovered more, but my opinions have been altered significantly over the course of 2015. Certainly the way in which I physically write is different; I got cancer in October and had an operation on my spine that left me immobile for a long while (meaning I now no longer write using a computer but type left-handed on a phone). But my actual views have changed, too. They seem to have become steadily more radical and I think I've become less shy about expressing them. Certain alterations also seem to have been quite random, and over the course of several months, I've identified as a Trotskyist, a Marxist-Leninist, a 'Left' Communist, and I'm fairly certain I was a Maoist at some stage. If you tracked the page on The Anonymous Revolutionary where I voice these views and opinions, you'd see that I can barely go a week without changing my mind as to which historical Marxist/Marxist ideology I relate to best.

The content has varied in a similar way. I started the blog with the tagline 'Marxism in the Modern World', and for the first four posts, I stuck religiously to current affairs and news stories, yet over time my blog became a lot more hypothetical, and I was more interested in drawing up a theory or proposing an idea than discussing the news with a socialist slant. I've also written posts where I simply talked about something Communist, like the short history of the Russian Revolution, and did once abandon Communism just to express a view (read How Language Legitimises Terrorism) using the justification of 'If I'm a Marxist expressing a political view, then it's effectively a Marxist view'. Marxism in the Modern World can thus be interpreted as anything from 'Hypothetical Marxist Ideas' to 'The Opinion of Someone who Happens to be a Marxist'.

This is why, when reading through the posts, you shouldn't assume anything is completely set in stone. I've looked back at older entries and seen myself express opinions I no longer hold or allude to something I no longer believe in. Perhaps it would be better to read this book as though it were documenting a journey, the development of several ideas: my views on Marxism, the world today, and the relationship between the two.

I'd like to say a word of thanks to all my readers and followers who experienced that journey first-hand, and to all the new ones I'm hopefully going to acquire. If I'm lucky, I may even indoctrinate some of you.

The Anonymous Revolutionary

1. CUBA: THE WORLD'S LAST ATTEMPT AT SOCIALISM

Posted on January 16, 2015

When the current thaw in US/Cuban relations made the news, it became clear that there were two sides to this debate. While many wanted to lift the embargo against the Cuban people, others undoubtedly wanted to starve the country's autocratic regime. I opposed these sanctions, but for an entirely different reason: I wanted to preserve what may be the world's last honest attempt at socialism.

On the opposite side of the globe, the Vietnamese Communist Party maintains firm leadership, yet what has truly become of Vietnam? A country, this is, where Coca-Cola is bought and sold as a consumer product – but it's not alone. The changes which such a country has seen are comparable to those which have taken place in the People's Republic of China, as within both China and Vietnam is a system driven and animated by force which seems to lie somewhere between Communist pride and nationalism, and perhaps some petty statement of reaching 'true socialism' through the market economies they have constructed for themselves in socialism's name. Given this is the world which the two nations have slipped into, will the current economic reforms concerning America's embargo against Cuba have the same consequences?

All I can say is that, given we're awfully short of Communist states, I hope not.

This will be a sensitive situation for many who lived under the repressive regime at the height of the Cold War, or even today, in a country where citizens have risked their lives to try and reach Florida, ninety miles away. The Black Book of Communism estimates that between 15,000 and 17,000 were killed under the regime, and (whatever the actual number) it's hard to imagine many friends, relatives or sympathisers of these victims supporting Barack Obama's decision to open the door to Cuba; I imagine they'd rather the United States continued to show no mercy and no remorse towards the regime in what the Lawton Foundation of Human Rights called an 'enslaved island'.

I'll accept that, but despite all this, I still believe that socialism should be given a chance. Not an illusion of socialism, but a full-blooded attempt. If, as a result of welcoming the United States, Cuba substitutes its own attempt with an illusion, as has been the case with both China and Vietnam, which nations will remain to keep the red flag flying? Even if one took for granted Marxist Economic Determinism – the theory of the proletariat inevitably leading the world to Communism due to their own exploitation; even if one maintained the belief that Communism is the final and inevitable truth, surely they'd accept that the sooner a nation such as Cuba arrived at that truth, the sooner the same would occur on a worldwide scale. If Cuba's attempt, which may well be the last attempt remaining, is thwarted by these reforms, this cannot happen.

I also want to talk about not just what Cuba is capable of achieving, but what it has already achieved. When discussing Communism with somebody opposed to it, they remarked that Cuba may be the only place where socialism has actually been partly successful. It is a country with free education, and not only free healthcare, but a healthcare system recognised internationally for its brilliance. According to the news source Al Jazeera, the infant mortality rate in the country is one of the lowest in the world, slightly lower than that of the United States, and life expectancy is over 77 years (among the world's highest).

Now Al Jazeera also states that the system which exists in Cuba is on the decline, but if this is what the country has constructed from autocracy, and political repression, imagine what the socialist regime, if truly developed, could construct. Just because Cuba is not currently at such a point it does not mean that this shall continue to be the case, and it definitely deserves a chance. Thus, when the end product is the possibility of achieving true socialism, along with the end of capitalist class-based oppression, sooner, the current existence of the autocratic Cuban state can be justified in Communism's name.

Finally, it is important to note that simply because the United States is no longer pretending Cuba doesn't exist does not mean liberty will prosper. Whether or not you'd be prepared to support autocratic socialism is really irrelevant, because, whilst in one circumstance socialism shall exist and in another it will not, autocracy will remain regardless (at least for the foreseeable future). As Senator Marco Rubio, a Floridian Republican and a child of Cuban immigrants said: "This entire policy shift announced today is based on an illusion, on a lie, the lie and the illusion that more commerce and access to money and goods will translate to political freedom for the Cuban people."

2. RUSSIA, CRIMEA AND PUTIN'S INTENTIONS

Posted on January 23, 2015

Have you ever considered the reasons behind the Russian invasion of Ukraine?

What drove Putin's order for the annexation of Crimea? Why did rebels in the east of the country attract Putin's attention? Why, when less than twenty-five years ago the Kremlin granted Ukraine its independence?

Feel free to disagree, but here's how I view the situation: the old KGB agent Vladimir Putin is now the president of a once revolutionarily heroic, progressive and promising nation at a point when the country could be viewed as directionless. Putin enters the stage after the collapse of the hope Communism once provided. Since 1991, though a great deal has probably improved, the country no longer even has a dream to hold onto.

I'll be honest. When I began this entry, the title I had in mind was 'Imperialism in the Russian Federation'. I was adamant that this entire issue was a matter of imperialist attitudes within 'Mother Russia'. However, my viewpoint changed today, when I read an article titled 'Ukraine and Crimea: what is Putin thinking?' on theguardian.com about an hour ago, explaining that 'Some have seen Putin's actions in the context of a post-imperial complex', and saying that 'There may be a flicker of truth in this, but the reality is more complex, according to those familiar with the Kremlin's decision-making over Crimea in recent weeks.' This got me thinking...

I came to the view that, regardless of the purely ideological perspectives one may view these events from; regardless of whether or not they ought to be labelled as 'imperialistic', one thing can't be denied: Putin needs Crimea for reasons outside the usual motives for occupation. The materialistic necessities for resources, the tactical necessities of territory to provide an advantage in battle, or perhaps the desire for the establishment of freedom or equality that drove the initial invasions of the Russian satellite states constituting the early Soviet Union – what could be seen as 'usual' motives for occupation, are not applicable to the situation.

It's clear that a state of this size and capability does not require Ukrainian influence

What I can make out from the events is this: Russia needs something to hold onto in the aftermath of Communism. Alongside the desire to remind the west of their capabilities and their superiority, a victory in Europe may provide a temporary solution to the air of dissatisfaction which has clouded the skies over Moscow since 1991. Clearly, without ever living in the country or having any real knowledge of the ideological perspectives within Russia, I can't say for definite, but the obvious benefit of the 'Communist dream's' collapse seems to be the fall of the autocratic Communist Party. Since then, however, one autocratic regime has been replaced with another, yet I think it's fair to say that the loss of an ideological dream has not been accounted for.

To provide a broader perspective on the situation, the article I'd previously referred to mentions the internal events in Ukraine, and the fact that Russia's influence on Ukraine was ceased by internal revolution, referring to one individual (Gleb Pavlovsky) who said that 'Putin hates revolution, he's a counter-revolutionary by nature.' In response to this, I'd say that obviously he wanted to re-establish his influence and did so by means of using and possibly assisting rebels (this is a matter open to debate), as well as annexing territory. I can't comment on Putin's own views on the concept of revolution, but I can say that I don't believe the Russian influence in Ukraine is truly necessary to Putin, and that the measures he took to secure it are, whilst a response to recent events, driven by internal desperation.

This is the conclusion I've come to: in a Russia devoid of the hope socialism provided, but with a still-stormy relationship with the western powers, and the autocracy Communism is so often blamed for, preserved, Putin's actions were rooted in his own desire to hold onto what he could. Thus, regardless of whether it was truly necessary in the longterm, his influence in that region was one he was not prepared to give up. I suppose, to see the truth (if we ever will), we'll have to wait and see how it all plays out.

3. TSIPRAS TAKES A STAND

Posted on January 31, 2015

Recently, as you probably know, the winner of the Greek election turned out to be the Socialist Party Syriza, or 'Coalition of the Radical Left'. The name is enough to suggest the ideological positions party members are coming from, as is the fact that their former Communist leader, Alexis Tsipras his named child Orpheus Ernesto, a possible tribute to Argentine revolutionary Che Guevara. Their economic stance, however, will be far more influential in the months to come: an opposition to austerity. When I first heard of them, I thought that their political and economic views clashed somewhat, given the nature of the organisation which they have sparked tensions within, this being the European Union.

I think we can all agree that the EU was founded on broadly leftist principles. Themes of proletarian internationalism can be seen within it, for example. This can be seen in the political climate in the United Kingdom (whose situation likely is to be similar to that of other countries) in that the debate on EU membership has assumed ideological characteristics: the Left support it, whilst a significant movement on the Right oppose it.

But the leader of the British Labour Party, Ed Milliband, according to the *Telegraph* newspaper, was once forced to deny that he was an 'old-fashioned socialist', highlighting the extent to which socialism in mainstream British politics has been watered down. Tsipras, on the other hand, whilst perhaps not reflecting the characteristics of the KKE (Communist Party of Greece), would obviously uphold and express far more radical views than Milliband. Yet what the Greek prime minister intends to bring to the scene of international politics was described by Andrew Smart, in an article published by the Idler Academy, as 'two fingers to the tyranny of the cult of productivity'.

It's this description that I'm interested in, as the conclusion I've come to is this: the European Union is no longer a leftist organisation. Whatever socialist principles it was founded upon have dried up with the current recession, and perhaps only the most moderate of Europe's contemporary Left see anything in the union any more. Jean-Claude Juncker does not strive for 'international justice' and 'economic liberation for the proletariat' or even any moderate imitations of true socialism: he wants to put an end to debt, and will happily wait for the countries of both Eastern and Western Europe, no matter how dismal or prosperous their economies, to pay. This will mean bad news for their citizens. A slogan used by the Communist Party USA, 'People and Nature before Profits', in my opinion, outlines a programme which the EU should adopt.

Tsipras is the first to take a significant stance, and I can only hope he's not the only one. I'd like to see this as the point at which the parties of Europe are beginning to realise that whilst debt presents significant concern, the demands of the people must come first. In any case, one can determine not only from the conditions causing the election result in Greece, but also the hostile attitudes it caused within the EU, the true nature of the organisation. Based in Brussels, the EU is currently an aloof bureaucracy centred on the elimination of debt at the cost of wellbeing, when it should learn to give more weight to people's urgent needs, especially in countries like Greece today.

4. REBELS IN YEMEN:
WHAT ARE THEY FIGHTING FOR?

Posted on February 8, 2015

Earlier this evening, when searching for a topic to write about, I came across reports about the recent events in the Arabian Peninsula.

For anyone unaware of what's happened, an insurrection has been carried out in Yemen by rebels known as the Houthis, sending a shockwave through the nation.

The Houthis are a rebel organisation, devoted to an area of Shia Islam known as Zaidism. Originating in the north of the country, they have been active, combating Al-Qaida forces in the region, for years. Recently, however, they have claimed a far greater prize: on 21st January, Houthi rebels overthrew the Yemeni government.

What actually occurred is as follows: as BBC News stated, in late January 'rebels stormed the presidential palace complex and put the president under house arrest', despite the signing of the peace deal on 21st September, after the rebel movement's occupation of Sana'a, the capital. Since then, President Hadi has resigned, and plans for the creation of a new government are underway.

President Hadi at the Pentagon in June, 2013

The causes of such a revolution are not clear, but the country has undergone years of corruption, political and economic instability and violence, and since the rebels (alongside their supporters) claim that the government has failed to address the situation, the rebellion may seem a rational move. I, however, am about to argue the opposite...

According to the Latin Post, after the Houthi insurgency, 'Thousands gathered in the centre of the city with placards calling for "Death to America, Death to Israel"'. The source also states that such a slogan has apparently become a Houthi trademark, and if this is the case, then it certainly gives the superficial impression of a radical and merciless band of fighters, not unlike the Jacobins in France or the Bolsheviks in Russia. After some research, however, it seems to me that the reality is somewhat different.

In studying the Houthis, I have found nothing which truly demonstrates an ideological or even political position. Their hatred for Zionism, Sunni Islam and American capitalism is evident, but that is all. Other than their attitudes towards certain conceptual ideas and their desire for immediate change, only their religious devotion is obvious.

I did gather information on their appeal within the country: Ian Black's article in the *Guardian* newspaper references April Alley, senior Arabian Peninsula analyst for the International Crisis Group, who commented the following: 'Supporters of the movement see the Houthis as correcting the wrongs of the country's 2011 transition agreement, which preserved the power and corruption of old regime elites.' She is also quoted as stating that 'They [supporters] praise the movement's willingness to confront corruption, combat Al-Qaida, and fill a security vacuum left by a feckless government.'

In my opinion, however, this is not enough, for we must not forget that the transition agreement occurred only three years ago, and that further unrest may well do as much to destroy its results as to preserve them. Even if the situation is exactly as the Houthis portray it, Hadi rose to power after the events of 2011, yet apparently this only led to circumstances similar to those which existed beforehand, and we have no reason to believe that the Houthis will not oversee the same occurring for a second time. In actual fact, there are reasons why Hadi may be the appropriate choice for the country: according to the Middle East Eye website, the UN Security Council 'backed Hadi as "the legitimate authority based on election results" and called on all parties and political actors in Yemen to stand with the government "to keep the country on track to stability and security."'

In any case, I do not believe that the Houthis, who seem to lack ideological basis and clear and specific direction, have a better claim to power than Hadi, whose intended transition to national 'stability and security' may be just as effective or perhaps even more so than that of the rebel movement, especially since the former has been given only three years to prove himself.

5. IF IT WASN'T FOR YELTSIN...

Posted on February 13, 2015

Today (Friday 13 February) according to HISTORYNET (http://www.historynet.com/today-in-history), was the day that Konstantin Chernenko, the second-to-last Soviet leader was selected as the successor to Yuri Andropov, as the Communist Party of the Soviet Union's General Secretary, in the year of 1984. To mark the thirty-first anniversary of this date, I thought that rather than focussing on a particular news story I'd write about the past, specifically the last days of the USSR, making it an appropriate time to address an interesting question: what would have become of the USSR if it hadn't been for its 1991 dissolution?

Even after the events of Christmas Day 1991, Communism, in the minds of many, doesn't seem to have departed. The current president is a former KGB agent, who referred to the Soviet Union's collapse as 'the greatest geopolitical catastrophe' of the century. Almost every city has a street named after Lenin, and whilst insignificant compared to the former Communist Party of the Soviet Union, the Communist Party of the Russian Federation remains strong and active.

In my opinion, the period of thaw under Khrushchev, whilst marking the height of the Cold War, paved the way for the collapse of Communism. I'd see this as a result of (I'll apologise in advance to any Stalinists) Stalin's reign, which brought famine, terror and repression on a scale incomparable to that under Lenin, the Provisional

16

Government or tsarism. And given that this is Russia we're talking about, a country with a long and bitter history of autocratic rule, it definitely says something. Even though the dismantling of Stalinism did not directly result in what is recognised as the 'Fall of Communism' (which, given what Stalinism actually implemented, was likely to be for the better) I believe it left behind a regime which was naturally inclined to thaw after Stalin's departure, eventually leading to its collapse.

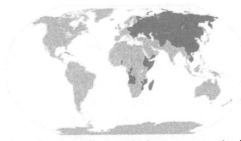

The coloured states constituted what was recognised as the Communist world at its height. Today, only a fraction of red states remain

Additionally, I believe Communism is not only dead for the present; it's remained dead for a significant period of time. The fall of the Soviet Union soon led to a return of capitalism in its constituent states, proving that Communism only survived in the area through the Communist Party of the Soviet Union, and as an idea rather than an actuality. Even Yugoslavia, a country independent (both nationally and politically) of the USSR, fragmented shortly after its dissolution, and only a handful of Communist countries remained around the globe.

But what if this hadn't occurred? What if Gorbachev had proved to be unsuccessful in the Soviet Union's dissolution, say, if the 1991 coup d'état had managed to preserve socialism? Would there still be an Eastern Bloc, an Iron Curtain, and firm alliances binding the first and second world into militarist organisations? During the extra twenty-four years, would the Communist world have expanded rather than declined?

To give an answer rather less dramatic than the question suggests it should be, I think not.

The way I see it, as I've already said, the Soviet Union had not seen socialism for a long while. The population may have caught a glimpse, in 1917, of where it might lie, but the efforts to reach it soon translated into bureaucracy, later totalitarianism. This resulted only in an illusion of socialism. In other words, if it weren't for Boris Yeltsin's government, I believe that any further efforts made by the Communist Party would have been simply buying time. By the 1990s, the once-so-tightly-enforced infrastructure had grown so fragile that protests and demonstrations occurred in Latvia, and the fears of the capitalist world were so weak that Gorbachev was able to announce the policy of 'Glasnost', and still retain power. If a new leader had decided to repress these Latvian demonstrators, or to preserve the hostility with Western Europe, I can't imagine the population would have tolerated it for long.

I've read that the Communist Party of the Russian Federation now promises Russia 'Chinese socialism', highlighting how desperate their situation really is.

In my entry on Cuba, I made it very clear what I believed Chinese and Vietnamese socialism to be: capitalism. If the leading Communist movement in a country which was once the world's first socialist state is resorting to watering down its philosophy in order to obtain votes, I don't think I need persuading that Communism has failed in Russia, and, in this particular format, is not likely to make a return anytime soon.

I conclude on this inglorious note by quoting a cropped version of the poem 'Goodbye Our Red Flag', from Yevgeny Yevtushenko's book *Don't Die Before You're Dead*.

Goodbye our red flag.
You slipped down from the Kremlin roof
Not so proudly
Not so adroitly
As you climbed many years ago
On the destroyed Reichstag
Smoking like Hitler's last fag.

Goodbye our red flag.
You were our brother and our enemy.
You were a soldier's comrade in trenches,
You were the hope of all captive Europe,
But like a red curtain you concealed behind you the Gulag
Stuffed with frozen dead bodies.
Why did you do it, our red flag?

Goodbye our red flag.
Lie down.

THE ANONYMOUS REVOLUTIONARY

Take a rest.
We will remember all the victims
Deceived by your sweet red murmur
That lured millions like sheep to the slaughterhouse.
But we will remember you
Because you too were no less deceived.

Goodbye our red flag.
Were you just a romantic rag?
Goodbye our red flag.
Pry open the fist
That imprisoned you
Trying to wave something red over Civil War
When scoundrels try to grab
Your standard again,
Or just desperate people,
Lining up for hope.

Goodbye our red flag.
You float into our dreams.
Now you are just a narrow stripe
In our Russian Tricolour.
In the innocent hands of whiteness,
In the innocent hands of blue
Maybe even your red colour
Can be washed free of blood.

Goodbye our red flag.
In our naïve childhood,
We played Red Army – White Army.

We were born in a country
That no longer exists.
But in that Atlantis we were alive.
We were loved.
You, our red flag, lay in a puddle
In a flea market.
Some hustlers sell you
For hard currency.
Dollars, Francs, Yen.

I didn't take the Tsar's Winter Palace.
I didn't storm Hitler's Reichstag.
I'm not what you call a 'Commie'.
But I caress the red flag
And cry.

— Thanks to Yevtushenko

6. MAO, XI AND THE WORST OF BOTH WORLDS

Posted on February 21, 2015

Thursday marked the Chinese New Year, and the beginning of the year 4713, making this an appropriate time to reflect on history and tradition, and a suitable(ish) time to talk about something that's been on my mind for a while: the politics and the economy of modern China.

The country, being the world's most heavily populated, is home to one of the largest armies, an ever-expanding economy and a haven of science and technology. Nowadays, it's even become fashionable to argue that China will soon overtake the United States in terms of power and world influence. Yet there is another side to the country, this being the political philosophy that drives its leaders: Communism.

So, if it's actually the case that China is not only experiencing great economic and military prosperity but has managed to achieve this through the means of a Communist economy, is China not a perfect example of a utopian socialist society?

If you've been reading my comments on China in previous entries, you'll know that the answer is, in my opinion, no. Finally, I have the opportunity to explain why...

To start with, let's look at the Chinese revolution, an act that would transform the country and the world, changing the shape of East Asia dramatically. The second independent

Communist state followed a similar path to that of Russia, its northerly neighbour: first the monarchy was overthrown by popular revolt (the Boxer Rebellion, or, in Russia's case, the February Revolution), then the bourgeois by Communist takeover (the Revolution of 1949, or the October Revolution) all with the help of an invasion from another imperialist country (Japan, or Germany) in the midst of an international war (World War Two, or World War One). Soon after, strict economic policies (the Great Leap Forward, or the Five Year Plans) were to be introduced, which would transform the economically backward peasant nations into giant industrial powers, at the cost of millions of lives. After the result was achieved and the chaos healed, relaxations in the policy followed (the thaw under Deng Xiaoping or Nikita Khrushchev), and the two nations progressed from then onwards. One major difference exists between Sino and Soviet Communism, however: the latter collapsed honestly whilst the former did not.

As I stated in my last entry, the period of thaw under Khrushchev gradually saw the withering away of the socialist state, setting the Soviet Union on a one-way road to its eventual dissolution. Strict economic regulations appeared to thaw after Mao's death, too, yet these reforms didn't lead to the state's downfall, only to the adoption of very relaxed, market-orientated policies, allowing China to succumb to what can only be described as 'sort-of socialism'. In other words, unlike the USSR, which collapsed honestly, openly rejecting the philosophy it was founded upon, Communist China retained its superficial character whilst the regime suffered internal destruction. To understand what this actually means for the Chinese people, we must examine conditions in China today, sixty-six years after the People's Republic of China was declared, under the leadership of Xi Jinping...

The initial problem 'sort-of socialism' presents in the case of China is that the socialist state is really nothing but an emerging capitalist one. Today, China is home to HSBC, Sinopec Limited, and many other brands, corporations and features we would regard as a central or vital aspect of the capitalist world. Whilst 'Made in China' may remain printed on the majority of everyday accessories, 'Designed in China' is becoming an equally suitable one. It's evident that, from what Deng Xiaoping referred to as 'Socialism with Chinese Characteristics', corporate empires have emerged, and thus the Chinese bourgeois, a class to whose elimination Mao dedicated his life, have been reborn.

It's not only the factory owners, however, who profit from the situation. China has a severe problem in deciding who, as a nation, it works for. Run by a government that claims the moral stance when it comes to justice for the proletariat, and a merciless stance when it comes to capitalist exploitation, the liberal capitalist west exploits labourers in China just as it does in Bangladesh and Indonesia. Many workers employed by the west produce iPads, iPhones, and iPods for little wages and long hours. In the country whose underdogs fought a bloody war to have their voices heard in the name of Communism, children toil in factories which have begun the process of installing giant nets outside the buildings to prevent successful suicide attempts, and in which workers are paid $1.50 per hour.

Astonishingly, the aspect of Chinese society which still exists according to socialist principles, the Communist leadership, simply allows both atrocities to occur. The Chinese Communist Party is perfectly capable of righting these wrongs; if he chose to, I'm completely confident that Xi Jingping could rid his nation of such oppression, and ensure that no factory worker ever worked under such conditions again. If they were truly devoted to the cause, I don't doubt that the party could even ensure a consistent, sufficient income for even the hardest-hit labourers.

Perhaps the thorough transformation of the Chinese economy akin to that of the Great Leap Forward would not be possible, or not without another several million deaths for the authors of the Black Book of Communism, and all their sympathetic readers, to wave in the face of Karl Marx and all his followers. After all, modern-day China has evolved this way, and their system of governance has developed into a capitalist one. Therefore I'd argue that Communism could no longer be reached without proletarian revolution. However, if the CPC wished to eliminate child labour, or to ensure justice for the workers who toil in the factories producing products to be sold globally, I'm confident that this would happen. Businesses would lose out in this scenario; China's economy might shrink; the western corporations (whom the Communist Party undoubtedly claims to despise in the first place) would lose a chunk of their overseas supply of workers, yet China could try and occupy a marginally-better position on the international scale of morality.

We must keep in mind that Mao Tse-tung, or Chairman Mao, fought a long civil war, introducing ruthless policies to combat counter-revolutionaries, and revolutionised the Chinese economy for a reason. I do not necessarily support such actions, and nor do I defend them, but if Mao was alive today, I'd be intrigued to see what he thought of modern-day China. Would he tolerate the exploitation currently in existence? Frankly, I can't imagine him doing so. I'd like to think that if nothing else, under Mao, the achievement of a proletarian dictatorship would have been wholeheartedly attempted.

It's important not to be deceived by the idea of a thawing China, for whilst Mao's legacy may have come to an end, authoritarianism, or perhaps even totalitarianism, has certainly not. The period of thaw consisted of the construction of an ever-expanding economy, or, in other words, the destruction of the socialist one Mao tried to achieve during the Great Leap Forward. Yet politically, China remains a highly censored and autocratic state. You only have to take a look at the persecution of those who practise Falun-Gong (a form of yoga) – something that would appear entirely unrelated to Communism, capitalism, or any issue which may concern the CPC – to be aware of the degree to which the Chinese people are tyrannised.

This is the reason why I believe the People's Republic of China is an embarrassment to socialism: it appears that the climate has been altered in one major way since Mao's leadership. That is to say that the state seems to have given up on achieving a true Communist society, leaving a country in which only the red flag, the party logo and the second 'C' in the party's name indicate a socialist society. It is clear that the autocratic bureaucracy has not shifted with the economic climate, upholding an authoritarian and tyrannical state which, whilst claiming a party name so untrue it would almost appear sarcastic, encourages the growth of a new bourgeois, thus creating the worst of both worlds. To put this into context, in Russia, 'Dictatorship of the Proletariat' soon gave way to regular dictatorship. In China, on the other hand, it has managed to transform itself into 'Dictatorship of the Bureaucrats and Those Who Happened to Benefit from Various Relaxations of Economic Policies, Partially Responsible (Alongside Foreign Exploitation Which the State Appears to Condone) for the Exploitation of the Chinese Workers'.

So there you have it. 'Sort-of socialism' is simply capitalism under the rule of an autocratic regime. No matter how hard they try, the Chinese Communist Party cannot justify their actions, or not, at least, in the name of Communism. China's political history, from Mao Tse-tung to Xi Jinping, is a history of injustice, tyranny and, despite the great industrial and technological advancements the country has made, failure.

7. ISLAMIC STATE FROM A WORLDWIDE PERSPECTIVE

Posted on February 28, 2015

In recent years fresh terror has arisen in the Middle East, as one of the most brutal organisations on the planet occupies vast areas in both Iraq and Syria. During 2014, recordings showing the decapitations of western journalists and reports highlighting the brutal treatment of local enemies began to increase tensions in the west. Now, as a great chunk of northern Syria and Iraq has fallen under the leadership of Abu Bakr al-Baghdadi, leader of the organisation, such tensions are higher than ever.

Islamic State (IS), also known as Islamic State of Iraq and Syria, Islamic State of Iraq and al-Sham, (ISIS), Islamic State of Iraq and the Levant (ISIL) or Islamic Caliphate, formed in 1999, and shares its roots with the infamous Al-Qaida. Since then, the organisation has committed many despicable acts, against both locals and foreigners. Reports showing the killings of westerners is one example, along with the fact that according to the *Moscow Times*, the group has openly declared war on the United States and, in a video depicting a member sitting in a military aircraft, threatened Russian president Vladimir Putin. The United States and Russia have had a bitter relationship for over half a century, and even since the end of the Cold War diplomatic relations have been precarious, especially with the current crisis in the Ukraine. IS, however, has taken the side of neither: they've even gone as far as to threaten both.

What does this say about the organisation's politics? Well, we can determine one thing: the fact that they'll always take their own side highlights the incompatibility of their ideology with the political systems of the world's powers, and for that matter, the rest of the world. No national army will fight alongside their forces, and yet IS continues to commit despicable acts independent of any other regime.

The haunting flag of this 'rouge terror'

Because of the brutality employed by the organisation, their lack of any real justification for their actions and their continuing hostility towards the rest of the world, this is an issue on which I feel the different powers of the world must put aside their differences to combat together. Left and Right, east and west, all states can share a common view-point on the organisation, and thus should all work to secure the safety of innocent civilians in Iraq, Syria and the bordering states, as well as in their own countries.

I've made my point clear, but I'll conclude the entry by addressing the leftists specifically: I feel that it's essential to understand IS in order to develop a rational answer as to how one should approach the issue, and so it must be made clear that the organisation is certainly not a socialist one, nor one fighting merely for justice or populism. This would seem obvious, but I imagine it would be easy for one to fall into the trap of believing that IS militants, existing in an area with a history of atrocities committed by multiple foreign powers (take the recent war in Iraq, or the Soviet invasion of Afghanistan, for examples), and one whose borders were drawn up by the western world, are actually combating imperialism.

It is definitely true that the area is subject to ongoing foreign mistreatment, including acts that could be considered disgraceful, and the fact remains that IS exists as a militant organisation opposing those who have treated the people in the region in such a way. This alone, however, does not mean that they fight to prevent these acts from being committed. It is essential to remember that as well as beheading journalists, they have terrorised the local population in a similar way. To give an example, the BBC News website states that an activist claims they have abducted up to 285 Christians in the Hassakeh province in Syria. The website also states that 'some 1,000 local Assyrian families are believed to have fled their homes in the wake of the abductions'. Even if other religions are taken out of the picture, their own religion and thus their central ideology (surely a community among which they would find solidarity) condemns IS, showing that they have no true ideological ground to occupy, and certainly no justification for their actions.

This is the reason why this debate is not a political one; there is only a moral and an immoral side. It is an issue on which all sensible individuals, no matter where they stand on the majority of political issues, should make the moral decision. Thus, on the question of IS militarism, Communists should come to the same conclusion as their capitalist opponents. It by no means requires an alliance with or respect for the capitalist world, rather the simple recognition that this is an issue which everyone, from both political extremes, should be able to agree on. Military intervention, on behalf of all those whom IS threatens, should seem the obvious conclusion.

8. THE RUSSIAN REVOLUTION IN NINE STAGES

Posted on March 7, 2015

Sunday will mark the ninety-eighth anniversary of the Russian February Revolution, as a consequence of which the tsar was overthrown in a flurry of populism, eventually leading to the Communist takeover the following October (November in the Gregorian calendar), and the rise of the world's first socialist state.

This is undisputedly one of the greatest moments of the twentieth century, on which so much history rests. The Cold War, the Cuban Missile Crisis, and the division of Germany, for example, would never have occurred had the revolution not taken place, and the same goes for the revolutions in nations like China and Cuba. Had Communism surfaced at all, it would have done so in drastically different circumstances, without the theoretical and practical guidance provided by Lenin, Trotsky and Stalin.

I won't lie; I've been wanting to write about this event since I began posting entries, and now that the anniversary of the occasion is (almost) upon us I have an excuse; I thought, in commemoration of the event, I'd post a short history of the Russian Revolution in nine, condensed stages.

So here goes...

1. The Final Years of Tsarism

Russia was the last absolute monarchy in Europe, and, stretching from the Baltic to the Chukchi Sea, the leadership of what Marx referred to 'the chief of European reaction', was struggling to maintain power over a steadily modernising population, growing ever more dissatisfied with conditions in the Russian Empire. The Romanov family had ruled the country for roughly 300 years, yet Nikolai II's reign was soon to draw to a close, marking the end of the monarchy altogether. But he wasn't easily broken; first, he had to endure a great number of uprisings, protests, and foreign aggression.

In 1904, the Russo-Japanese war broke out. Despite Russian military superiority, the conflict resulted in a Japanese victory, which coincided with what later became known as the Failed Revolution of 1905. What occurred didn't have anywhere the impact of the events in 1917, but could well have done, if circumstanceshad been different. One key difference between the revolt of 1905 and that of the February Revolution was that the latter had gained the support of the army, whilst the former had not, which could well have been the primary reason why it didn't achieve what it planned to.

In any case, Nikolai watched the revolution's defeat at the hands of the military, and continued his reign. In order to ease the growing tensions, he signed the October Manifesto, promising change, and thus created the Duma, a legislature which would limit the extent of his power. Nonetheless, he was naturally opposed to reform, and quoted as saying 'I cannot squander a legacy that is not mine to squander.' He may well have signed the manifesto only in order to prevent a second revolution, which he might have realised would be, as it eventually was, successful.

2. War, Women and Industrialisation: the Causes of the February Revolution

In spite of the reforms following the events of 1905, Nikolai could not secure his own autocracy. Perhaps this wouldn't have been the case if it hadn't been for the greatest conflict of the twentieth century: World War One. Personally, I believe that if the army had not been involved in such a war, neither the revolutionary movement in February nor the

Bolsheviks in October would have gained popularity, or at least not on the massive scale in which they did so.

Having just endured the war with Japan and the revolution of 1905, and now (as the leader of a nation bound to France and Britain by the Triple Entente) on the brink of a global conflict, Nikolai waged total war, and many suffered as a consequence (the majority of which were peasants, who comprised 85% of the Russian population).

Simultaneously, the industrialisation which took place throughout the Russian Empire may have been to the Tsar's disadvantage. The expanding industrial proletariat provided a basis for Communism, perhaps directing or at least contributing to Russia's evolution beyond the post-February period, since the Bolsheviks found their bastion of support in the industrial proletariat. Railways were constructed, too, which contributed to the revolutionary cause in an entirely different and unforeseeable way, as the railway and transport lines were seized on the night of the October Revolution.

On February 23rd (Julian calendar), many partook in a demonstration in Petrograd (Saint Petersburg), the then capital of Russia, for International Women's Day and in protest against bread shortages, an event which was followed by strikes and other protests in the city. Realising that what was unfolding in front of them had the potential of over-throwing the Russian monarchy altogether, the Mensheviks (the moderate wing of the defunct Russian Social Democratic and Labour Party, after the party split into the Bolshevik ('majority') and Menshevik ('minority') factions), established the Petrograd Soviet. Soviets (elected councils) existed throughout the Russian Empire, but this one's role was significant; it existed with the intent of directing revolution.

Meanwhile, Nikolai was visiting troops on the frontline, and on hearing of the events in Petrograd, ordered his own soldiers to fire upon the crowds of protesters. The real trouble occurred at that moment, as many of the soldiers sympathised more with the crowds than with the tsar, and so joined in, often firing directly at police officers. As he no longer had the support of the army, Nikolai could not quash the revolt, and so abdicated, ending the 300-year Romanov dynasty of Russia.

3. From Populism to Socialism: the Rise of the Bolsheviks

Much happened in the period after the February Revolution that would change Russia for ever. The Provisional Government, a temporary parliamentary body comprising many members of the tsar's former parliament, assumed leadership, but overall power was shared between two movements; after the revolt, Russia entered a period known as Dual Power, referring to an effective coalition between the Provisional Government and the Petrograd Soviet. The popular demands were, to some degree, met, yet Dual Power existed only for eight months (before a second revolution was carried out). Nonetheless, the period in which Russia was in such a state marked some of the most dramatic changes seen in the nation's history.

As the New Year progressed, whatever liberal intentions the Provisional Government had were being increasingly overshadowed by their autocratic and conservative policies. Whilst they declared an amnesty for all political prisoners charged prior to the revolution, they refused both Poland's and Finland's appeal for independence. Whilst they addressed the 'people of the whole world', stating their demand for peace and calling for an end to the war, they made no efforts to stop the war effort. In fact it was partly the issue of war which worked to determine the government's fate: the news that Russia was promised the straits at the Black Sea's mouth were she to be militarily victorious sparked major protests.

Throughout February, Russia's future leader watched from a distance. Vladimir Illych Ulyanov, or Lenin, was exiled in Switzerland due to his revolutionary activities. There, he would write the April Theses, denouncing an alliance with the Provisional Government and insisting upon a second, socialist revolt, a demand which was to change the face of the revolutionary movement entirely. He returned shortly thereafter, smuggled onto a train to Russia, and from that moment on, he was able to influence Russian politics directly. Another side to the revolution – the radical Left –, was about to emerge.

Upon his return, the Bolsheviks (the party of which he was the leader) grew massively in numbers. Many workers joined the Bolsheviks without knowledge of the party's political stance, yet realising the support they would provide for the working people. If it hadn't been for the sudden growth in membership, it could be argued that the party would not have had the national recognition to successfully take control of the country later that year. As the significance of the Bolsheviks grew, distinguishing the party from the other faces in the revolutionary crowd, the popularity of the Provisional Government declined. This became clear during the July Days, when anti-war protesters were fired upon by soldiers under the government's leadership. What fuelled the protest was the fact that the new prime minister, Alexander Kerensky, had just conducted a failed offensive resulting in the death of roughly 20,000 Russians.

Meanwhile, the other revolutionary parties were divided over whether to continue fighting Germany – this also worked in Lenin's favour. The Socialist Revolutionaries, for example, split into Right and Left factions; the Right SRs, as they became known, supported the war effort whilst the Left, who occupied similar ideological ground to the Bolsheviks and would later become their coalition partner, opposed it. Many in the country, after enduring years of misery brought about by external conflict, grew sympathetic towards Lenin's cause.

Come October, the Bolsheviks were a leading party in Russia, capable of staging revolution, and it was evident that the Provisional Government didn't embrace or act on behalf of the populist movement that had brought down the former regime, providing them with a noble cause. Lenin acknowledged the government's true colours early on, and whilst in

Switzerland (only two months after they assumed power), he stated that there should be no support or alliance with them. Once again, Russian capitalism was about to suffer catastrophic defeat, which was to prove fatal this time.

4. One Night in October...

The patrol of the October Revolution

Two revolutions make up what we know as the '1917 Russian Revolution': one occurred in February, the other, in October. The October Revolution is perhaps the more famous of the two, partly because of its significance in marking the birth of the world's first socialist state, the Russian Soviet Federative Socialist Republic (RSFSR). As it successfully brought down the Provisional Government, this revolution could be seen to be completing the tasks of February. One key difference between the two, however, was that the October revolution was coordinated; what occurred in February was a popular uprising, which, whilst directed and supported by many parties (specifically the Mensheviks and the Socialist Revolutionaries) was not sparked or led by any; yet in October, the overthrow of the government took place in the form of an organised coup d'état.

On the night of October 25th, or November 6th in the Julian calendar, the Bolsheviks, Red Guards (soldiers assisting the Bolshevik cause) and Kronstadt sailors stormed the Winter Palace, with a shot fired from the ship *Aurora* serving as the signal. Although protected by the Women's Battalion, the palace was poorly defended, allowing the seizure of power to occur. On the same night, the Bolsheviks took control of railway lines, along with other crucial locations in the city of Petrograd, effectively seizing the capital's infrastructure.

Even though it is referred to as the Great October Socialist Revolution, it's worth noting that it was significantly less dramatic than what one might have expected. It was almost bloodless, was carried out by only a handful of devoted revolutionaries, and in the space of just twenty-four hours. Come the following morning, however, the new regime, which was to last up until Gorbachev's leadership in the early 1990s, would take its first breath.

5. A Nation Divided

**A stamp depicting a soldier in the Red Army,
marking the 20th anniversary of its creation**

Soon after November 6th, the political situation entered a period of crisis. Those who were to form the volunteer armies constituting the Russian 'White Army' opposed socialism from the start, yet the Mensheviks and Socialist Revolutionaries, two parties considered to be central to the February Revolution and the post-February period, were quickly alienated from Russian socialism, leaving the Bolshevik regime on the verge of collapse. One reason for this was the dissolution of the Constituent Assembly, which omitted the moderate socialists from government.

This was a body of elected representatives forming a coalition government, created shortly after the October Revolution, when the Russian population participated in what is considered the first ever practice of democracy in the country. The election was called by Lenin, who had frequently criticised the Provisional Government's refusal to do so. Thus, when he assumed power, he had no choice but to do so himself. In the election the Bolsheviks received only a quarter of the vote, despite being the most popular party among workers and soldiers. The assembly met only once, as it was dissolved by Lenin after the Socialist Revolutionaries (the winners of the election) refused to accept the Bolsheviks' ideas on issues such as soviet power.

As a result of both this and many other unpopular actions committed by the party, and the ideological opposition they faced, they soon grew very unpopular. War broke out almost instantly, and the White Army fought as a voluntary militarist movement against the Bolsheviks. Consequently, the Red Army (founded and led by former Menshevik Leon Trotsky) grew significantly in numbers to the point where it became the largest organ of the state, consuming a large proportion of funds and almost draining the Russian economy. After several years of fighting, the result was a red victory, but how and why this occurred is a more complex matter.

A contributing factor was organisation: the Red Army was efficient and well disciplined, fighting for a Communist Russia (under Trotsky's autocratic leadership, discipline even extended to decimation within the ranks in order to eliminate conspiracy). Meanwhile, the White Army fought for 'Russia: One and Indivisible', in other words, the existence of an Orthodox Christian country, operating in a similar fashion to the pre-revolutionary empire. They were largely nationalistic and conservative, sharing similar views on most areas, but, as a voluntary army, they lacked direction and failed to organise themselves sufficiently.

On top of this, the Red Army fought for the state, yet existed only as one of multiple state organs. In other words, the Bolsheviks could defeat the Whites through other means. The Cheka (Bolshevik secret police) was one, and the programme it carried out, known as the Red Terror, worked to eliminate dissidence through political persecution. Opponents of the regime were hanged, shot or imprisoned. The White Army carried out the White Terror, but since their members had the sole resort of militarism, this consisted only of the brutality exemplified by their fighting forces.

Although the Bolshevik regime almost collapsed, the events of this period actually assisted the state in many ways. Namely, they worked to polarise political views, eliminating the moderate socialists who had become alienated from the radical Left after October, for the conflict was very much a battle between Reds and Whites. Those occupying the middle ground had to choose a side, that of the Red Army (who, at the very least, would fight to defend the revolution), seeming the logical option, or they were reduced to insignificance. This was due to multiple reasons, but strategy played a key role: they were less inclined to resort to brutality, yet couldn't fight effectively without doing so. Whatever the reasons, they became less of a threat as that of radical counter-revolutionaries grew.

The war finally drew to a close and the Bolsheviks emerged even stronger and more ruthless than before. They operated bureaucratically, and hierarchy quickly developed within the party, whilst their grip on the populace tightened into strict authoritarian rule. This is probably a consequence of the tragic events brought about by counter-revolution, both during and after the war, and the awareness of the regime's insecurity due to threats from the outside world. Prior to 1917, for example, it was possible that the party was aiming to create a politically liberal society, yet this changed dramatically following the revolution. When an opponent once challenged Lenin's policies, advocating the right to freedom of speech, Lenin's responded by stating that 'we are not going to commit suicide!'

6. War Communism and the Russian Economy

Victims of the 1921 famine

The economic strategy adopted by the Bolsheviks became known as War Communism, which consisted of a strictly centralised economy, in which commerce was made illegal and all means of production were nationalised. It is unknown whether such a format was introduced to achieve true Communism, or as a pragmatic solution to the economic crisis Russia was submerged in.

The state's complete and utter control over all means of production can be seen most clearly in the policy's effect on the peasantry, who had their grain seized. They hoped that it would be repaid later, but we now know this wasn't the case. Much of the grain that they relied upon as a food source was used for other purposes – none of it was returned.

The result of this was a famine in which millions died, and the necessity for intervention by the west (the American Relief Administration was a significant contributor). The implementation of a policy which even banned the word 'trade' also gave rise to a fresh wave of state dissidents, and those who refused to hand over their grain were punished.

Eventually, the catastrophic effects of the policy were too great, even for Lenin, and a separate policy was introduced, known as the New Economic Policy (NEP). The fact that such a significant change had been made to the country's economic system highlights the true nature of War Communism, for Lenin wasn't somebody to give up, especially when the matter concerned socialism. Yet this issue was different: he recognised that if he was to maintain leadership he would need to adapt to the climate.

Despite the need to adjust policies, many believed that the NEP was simply a reintroduction of capitalism into the economy, and rejected the idea that it should be implemented in a Communist Russia. Supporting such an argument is the fact that, under the policy, several small businessmen (the NEP men) were able to profit in a manner akin to that in the free-enterprise economy before the revolution.

The policy itself was fairly relaxed in comparison, and permitted free-enterprise capitalism to operate on a small scale. Whilst the NEP was mocked as the 'New Exploitation of the Proletariat', and its introduction invited criticism of Lenin by more 'radical' Communists, it served its purpose in kick-starting the Russian economy, since, at this point, production had dropped below pre-revolutionary levels.

7. The Formation of the Soviet Union

Central to the concept of Marxism is the idea of global revolution, and the Bolsheviks recognised this from the start. Thus, their invasions of the neighbouring territories soon followed their rise to power. The Soviet Union would only be the starting point, and once Communism was established it would spread on a worldwide scale.

The Soviet Union, or formally, the Union of Soviet Socialist Republics (USSR) consisted initially of Russia and the surrounding states, including modern-day Kazakhstan, Ukraine and Belarus. The fact that Russia had previously established an empire in the region probably assisted their cause in the invasion; if such an empire had never existed, nationalism (which had been suppressed in these nations during the days of empire) might well have restricted the Red Army significantly.

Nationalism, as a movement, did actually help to compromise the invasion somewhat, for the Bolsheviks were originally opposed to the idea of federalism; they only accumulated the Russian satellite states after drawing borders around ethnic groups and former nationalities. Nonetheless, the Red Army covered significant ground, marching beyond the Russian borders, establishing not just one, but a union of Communist states.

It is worth noting that, Communism wasn't popular among the workers of the eastern world. There was a time when a French Communist newspaper, *L'Humanité* was the most widely read newspaper in the country, when many in the west admired the USSR and the principles on which it stood, and when Communist revolutions in countries such as Germany (which did very nearly occur) were not only anticipated but expected. In fact, after the Bolsheviks took power, the proposal to continue the war effort against Germany, with the hope of establishing a revolutionary German state, received four votes; while Lenin's proposal for peace received seven. If this hadn't been the case, or if the European Left had pursued a more militant strategy, the borders of the USSR might have been drastically different.

8. Post-1924 Tensions and the Rise of Stalin

An informative poster explaining Lenin's death

Lenin, the leader of the Bolsheviks, died of a stroke in 1924.

Just before his death, he wrote a testament, which was, as Trotsky said 'Lenin's last advice on how to organise the party leadership'. One particularly perceptive recommendation he made was that Stalin should be removed from his post within the party 'to prevent a split' from occurring – something we know is exactly what happened following his death. Prior to this point, differences of opinion had divided the party into obvious factions; moderates such as Rykov had feuded with Lenin on certain issues, and Lenin had feuded with the Left on others. Yet the party always remained unified, perhaps because always existed under a common leadership.

When that leader died, however, tensions began to surface, becoming evident in the power struggle that followed. It could also be argued that before this point, the Bolsheviks had found themselves too of situations either dire or important for any real rivalry to occur. Before October, they planned the Communist revolution and in the manner in which it would take place. Shortly after, civil war had broken out, and fighting continued until 1924. Naturally, differences of opinion often sparked disagreement and debate, yet the 'split' which Lenin had warned of had not yet occurred.

Another factor that may not have been foreseen, except perhaps by Lenin, was Josef Stalin's steady rise to power. It would seem, in retrospect, that he wanted nothing but authority and strove to achieve it. Stalin established alliances within the party, siding with different members at different times for tactical purposes. He also led the mourning at Lenin's funeral, and, in an attempt to disgrace Trotsky, his greatest opponent within the party, told him the wrong date for the occasion. First he sided with the Left, to weaken moderates like Bukharin, then with Bukharin to compromise the 'Left Opposition' (Trotsky, Kamenev and Zinoviev). Eventually, after he and Bukharin won the power struggle, he took control of the party and sided with neither faction, expelling those who opposed him, constructing a personality cult around himself and transforming the party apparatus drastically, as I shall now explain…

9. The Red Tsar

Russia took a sudden turn away from reform under Stalin's leadership: the NEP was replaced by forced collectivisation, and the liberal and progressive attitudes of the Bolshevik Party, which legalised homosexuality, abortion, no-fault divorce, and promoted the emancipation of women, were replaced by far more conservative ones. Reliance upon the use of the gulag network increased, along with the degree of censorship employed by the party, and authoritarianism slipped into dictatorship as his power increased steadily.

The 'Red Tsar', as he is sometimes referred to, actually demonstrated a sympathy for the reactionary views of the tsars before him, and on the question of brutality, demonstrated a capability and a passion far greater than any of them. Stalin also took actions which could be seen in contradiction to Marxism, such as the practice of 'Socialism in One Country', an idea he proposed in opposition to the Marxist concept of world revolution. Unlike the first Soviet Republics, he established the Communist states of Eastern Europe as more of a buffer zone than anything else. In what was largely an attempt to consolidate power, the majority of old Bolsheviks were also purged under Stalin's regime, and his old opponent Trotsky, who had been exiled and resided in Mexico, was assassinated alongside most of his family.

Stalin's actions, viewed critically by the majority of the world gave rise to an ongoing debate as to whether they were the product of Stalinism alone, or the inevitable outcomes of Bolshevism. A viewpoint known as the totalitarian model argues that Stalin's leadership merely exemplifies what Communist rule would have unquestionably come to, and that the atrocities for which he is blamed – the terror, the strict economic centralisation and the rise of the police state – would have been committed by the government regardless of who won the power struggle. The alternate viewpoint – the revisionist model – argues that Stalin alone is responsible for the chaos he caused, that this period of history, a particularly fluid and unpredictable point in time, could have given rise to a completely different form of leadership. After all, the principles that drove Russia to revolution, also the underlying principles of Bolshevism, were not those of authority, order and obedience but freedom and equality.

Another frequently raised question is whether or not Stalin betrayed Lenin, who did, we mustn't forget, recommend that Stalin left the party before he died. Obviously, links can be seen between the Stalinist terror and the Bolshevik Red Terror, which was enacted on Lenin's orders, perhaps between Stalin's policy of collectivisation and that of War Communism, also implemented under Lenin. But on the other hand, marked differences can be seen between the two. Lenin was not noticeably power-obsessed, for example, he sought to end racial antagonisms when Stalin is accused of promoting them (Stalin has been frequently accused of antisemitism), and he upheld liberal and progressive views when Stalin did not. As I've said, Stalin was unusual in this respect, as, unlike many other Bolsheviks, his social beliefs orientated him to the right. An unlikely advocate of Russian nationalism, the Georgian revolutionary incorporated patriotic ideas into the Communist regime when Lenin would never have done (this being an area in which such betrayal is obvious) though he nonetheless managed to effectively combine political conservatism with economic socialism, very definitely taking Lenin's contributions on board. As the historian Steve Smith said in 'The Russian Revolution: A Very Short Introduction', Stalinism 'synthesized many elements of the Russian national tradition with Leninism, its character as a mobilizing party-state making it very much a creature of the 20th century.'

I would recommend Smith's book for further reading on this subject.

9. THE COMMERCIALISATION OF COMMUNISM

Posted on March 13, 2015

Best part about them: Made in China

Since everything I've posted so far is fairly dense, I thought I'd post something slightly more light-hearted. It would make a perfect opportunity, I've decided, to address an issue that's been on my mind lately: if Communism exists to dismantle the capitalist mode of production, and tear down every corporate empire on the face of the earth, then when and why has Communist imagery found its way into the market?

The jokes surrounding Che Guevara T-shirts are an example of the extent to which this is happening, yet the printing and selling of these T-shirts, whilst perhaps so, well, blatantly *wrong* to have attracted attention, is not the only example. The market today is full of these products, from Commie Mints to Maoist messenger bags, and they're not always where you'd expect. Whilst the postcards shown above were bought from the DDR Museum in Berlin, the T-shirt came from a village market in the south of France and the mints from a branch of the sweet shop Candy Hero.

The deliberate commercialisation of such icons is actually just the start, for images such as the red star have been sold in a subtler way, probably without deliberately selling the Communist associations they have. It just goes to show the variety of meanings these images can possess, all depending on the person viewing them: even to the extent to which they become corporate branding techniques and icons used by anti-corporatist revolutionaries.

Yet what really puzzles me is how the capitalist world can endorse Communist imagery in such a way. Yes, it's joked about, but not in a way that seems nearly sufficient given what the industry is actually doing. It also seems as if, by promoting the ideas of revolution, even in the shallowest sense possible, the capitalists are advertising the struggle against capitalism itself. Yet I think the manufacturers (who would probably rather view themselves as people simply building their own business and making a living, rather than a link in the global capitalist network) are probably too short-sighted to care.

In any case, I certainly believe that whoever has managed to pull this off deserves a reward. Nothing in the Communist world, not even the Stalinist regime of terror and political repression, claiming to act in the interests of socialism – and thus humanity – has managed to get away with such blatant irony. Those behind the manufacturing of these products have exemplified something fascinating: they have clearly demonstrated capitalism's remarkable ability to sell you absolutely anything, even the face of its greatest opposition.

10. IMPERIALISM, ISOLATIONISM AND COMMUNISM

Posted on March 20, 2015

The way I see it, all Communist states (and in fact, all Communists) embrace elements of one of the following ideas: isolation or imperialism. Which one exactly depends on the conditions of the state or the individual concerned, yet both can be exemplified, which seems odd, as both are unpopular ideas within the Communist movement.

National isolation is an idea which Communism has frowned upon for multiple reasons. Such a rule cannot be applied to every situation, yet in general, the separation of one portion of the proletariat through the artificial division of states can be seen in contrast to class struggle, especially since Marx himself believed the nation-state was a bourgeois creation. In the Communist Manifesto, it is written that 'National differences and antagonism between peoples are daily more and more vanishing, owing to the development of the bourgeoisie, to freedom of commerce, to the world market, to uniformity in the mode of production and in the conditions of life corresponding thereto. The supremacy of the proletariat will cause them to vanish still faster.'

Equally, Communism rejects imperialism – the practice of constructing an empire – probably more profoundly so. This can be seen most clearly from a Maoist (Third-Worldist) perspective, known for its fierce opposition to the exploitation of the third world by nations of the first, perhaps even more so than to labour exploitation in general. Even outside of Maoism, one would struggle to identify an openly imperialist advocate of Marxism. Long before Mao's theories gained significance, Vladimir Lenin referred to imperialism as the 'Highest phase of capitalism', probably eliminating all prospects of its official establishment among the Communist world.

The prospect is simple: both ideas appear counter-revolutionary in the field of Marxism. Yet, if you examine the Communist and formerly Communist world, it appears that every state will have fallen into one of these traps...

The reason for this is as follows: I believe that the following two theories have split Communism down the middle more drastically than any others: world socialism, and Socialism in One Country. This division has its roots back in the Bolshevik power struggle of the 1920s, in which Trotsky, an outspoken internationalist, talked of spreading the revolution, whilst Stalin spoke of cultivating Russian

Communism independent of the outside world. Stalin's ideas proved far more influential, for the majority of socialist states seem to have followed the path of building socialism independently. Thus, as independent Communist states in a capitalist world, they took an increasingly isolationist approach, setting themselves apart from their neighbours. Often, this led to the rise of heavily nationalistic views within the regime, as has been the case in various Communist states across East Asia.

By contrast, the Communist world has also embraced ideas of world socialism, which can be seen again in the example of the USSR (prior to Stalin's leadership), which existed not as one nation, but as a network of states bound together by the common leadership of Moscow. Critiques of such a system highlight the fact that this was achieved by the repression of what have become known as the Russian 'satellite states', reducing them to mere provinces in the power block and thus robbing them of the national identity they once possessed. This has been criticised as an imperialist idea, for obvious reasons, causing countries like the early Soviet Union to acquire negative connotations. So there you have it: at one end of the spectrum you have Lenin's Soviet Union, and on the other, North Korea. As a Communist country is, by nature, an enemy of the international capitalist world, a revolutionary state has two choices: it can fight capitalism, or it can hide from capitalism. Either way, it involves going to one of two extremes, for (not including the westernised and, let's be honest, post-Communist nations like China) they can't just simply exist, but either extreme entails an ugly scenario.

11. RUSSELL BRAND AND
THE BRITISH REVOLUTION

Posted on March 27, 2015

About a century ago, the majority of the British population earned their bread by toiling long hours in factories, only just able to keep themselves afloat, in the grasp of the obscenely wealthy bourgeoisie. Where disaffection would appear commonplace and poverty was accepted as the standard, proletarian rebellion, even Communist revolution on the streets of Manchester or East London, would have seemed entirely possible. So much so, in fact, that Marx himself regarded England as the most likely setting for such a revolution to occur.

Today, the small island off the north-western coast of Europe is certainly a changed one. The traditional image of the London Docklands as a sprawling mass of smog-ridden factories has been replaced by that of an economically prosperous, thriving-market metropolis. The idea of socialist revolution today may seem ridiculous, but recently, a whole new wave of 'revolutionary' populism has arisen.

Who are these twenty-first-century revolutionaries? And, more importantly, who exactly are they fighting for?

Russell Brand, the actor and comedian recently ranked the fourth most influential thinker by *Prospect* magazine, has become a voice of revolution in the United Kingdom, an idea that attracts many. Leftist culture has always been present among the student population, yet today it seems that radical ideas have taken a turn worth mentioning. Now, individuals like Brand, alongside 'Anonymous', a network of associated activists, have taken to protest and public demonstration. Against what, it isn't always clear, but their broadly liberal and socialist aims seem to point to something larger than their cause, this being a general shift in attitude, with radicalism starting to make a slow reappearance in the country.

Anonymous' signature logo portrayed in the form of street art

As I've previously mentioned, our capitalist enterprise was, not so long ago, a worker-dominant state under the shackles of the capitalist giants. Such a transformation, from that to the present one, was made peacefully, during the process of 'de-industrialisation'. These demonstrations, however, are small reminders that the revolutionary culture has not deserted society. And of course, every revolution needs a target, so once again we are forced to realise that the achievement of human rights, liberty and justice for the oppressed in Britain is by no means complete.

Yet should it be the task of Russell Brand and his like to complete it?

I recently came across an organisation in the UK known as the Revolutionary Communist Group (RCG), who, in a video, pointed out that the Labour Party has betrayed socialism and no longer represents the working class as a whole. Now, this 'revolutionary' movement has embraced populism in a similar manner, and it's just a case of whether or not they will do justice to those they represent. Today, I don't feel I need to spend a great deal of time discussing why the Labour Party in Britain has turned its back on true leftism, an issue on which I agree with the RCG. Will the new branch of 'revolutionaries' do the same? Judging by their superficiality, their lack of direction or dogmatism, and their somewhat casual attitude towards the revoution, I'd say so.

Whilst the Labour Party clearly demonstrates such misrepresentation, I believe it's only one example; whilst Britain has been entirely transformed over the past century, it seems those who truly deserve justice have simply been transferred from one manner of life to the next, with their political and social representation taken care of by those above them in the economic pecking order. If anybody wants to see a difference made to British society similar to that which these liberal and socialist organisations advocate, this must change. Revolution must lose its superficially attractive shine, and activism must ake on genuinely motivated qualities.

Though I don't necessarily believe members of other classes cannot partake in or assist the socialist movement (if this was the case, how would movements such as the Bolsheviks in Russia have managed to seize power?), we could learn a lesson from Karl Marx, who stated that 'the emancipation of the working class must be the work of the working class itself'. If such an idea was applied in Britain, real change might just occur.

12. THE THIRD 'BLOC' THAT NEVER HAPPENED: TITO AND THE NON-ALIGNED MOVEMENT

Posted on April 3, 2015

The idea of socialism outside of the Eastern Bloc has surfaced multiple times in history, perhaps most famously among the Communist Left, and later the followers of Mao Tse-tung or, to a lesser extent, Che Guevara. It will have undoubtedly intrigued many intellectuals and revolutionaries since the birth of the USSR, one of whom I will focus on in particular...

Josip Broz Tito, the Croatian-born leader of Yugoslavia, did something both extraordinary and somewhat reckless, which, I've decided, shall be the subject of this entry: he led the first state in Eastern Europe, then in the grip of Soviet influence, to become 'socialist, but independent'.

What relevance does this have? Well, April is the month which, twenty-three years ago, saw the breakup of the Socialist Federal Republic of Yugoslavia. On April 28th, 1992, Serbia (the last of the Yugoslav republics) became an independent nation, serving as the final nail in the coffin for the great Communist federation of south-eastern Europe. This was a country fundamentally different from many others: it was among the first to have been liberated by the Red Army, yet to reject the USSR, and operated under the system that could have been described as 'council Communism', where workers' councils and unions would provide the basis for socialist transformation, which could be seen in contrast to that of the Soviet Union.

Yet equally interesting are the social and political ideas of international socialism that Marshal Tito upheld, for he was an active member, and later leader, of the Non-Aligned Movement. This is an ongoing organisation representing the interests of developing countries, with the founding aim of 'opposing imperialism and neo-colonialism, especially from western domination'. Such an idea was most apparent in the Cold War's polarisation of political identities, with the desire to create an 'independent pathway' for these states so that they would adhere to neither the USA nor the USSR.

I'll say this now: this entry is not an opinionated one; I won't go into depth about my personal views on the subject or on the political views of Tito generally. Rather, I'm writing to discuss this idea of an 'independent pathway', and its relevance to both Communism and capitalism.

The movement's member states

Coming back to the Cold War, it couldn't have been a more interesting time to consider a third power arising in the world, combating both the Eastern and Western blocs with a newly developed idea of proletarian internationalism. It also provided an opportunity to oppose what could have been perceived as Soviet imperialism (a particular criticism which did gain a degree of popularity) whilst remaining true to the principles of Communism. In other words, you would no longer have to bear the label of 'Soviet sympathiser' to consider yourself a Communist.

In the latter half of the previous century, however, history seems to have had other ideas. The two 'blocs', the great realms of power, split Europe down the middle in much the same way that the Triple Entente and the Triple Alliance had divided the continent at the beginning of the twentieth century, only such a division was far clearer easily distinguishable now that it adopted political connotations. Yet it was surely obvious that such a scenario, that is, Europe's division into a Communist east and a capitalist west, could never have been a permanent situation, making the formation of a third power bloc perfectly possible. Why then, in a climate of hate and tension, when a third way was definitely on the cards, didn't this new union form?

I've been thinking, and here are the reasons I've managed to come up with:

Five Reasons Why the 'Third Bloc' Never Arose

1. A lack of information on Marxist philosophy or Communism as a political theory within these countries (especially in the less well-developed nations).
2. A lack of the necessary conditions for Communist revolution due to less-advanced methods of production.

3. The development of a view of both west and east as 'similarly evil' threats to these nations and cultures, without adequate consideration of the political climate, and thus the demand for the national sovereignty against the two powers compromising proletarian revolution.

4. The division of these nations by the two powers, directing them against each other and against the respective power blocs, as the west's and the east's spheres of influence adapt the political climate of these countries to their immediate needs, an example of which would be the United Kingdom's influence over the former British colonies.

5. The tendency of the division separating the capitalist and the Communist worlds to polarise political thought worldwide, rendering the construction of a third power increasingly difficult.

While we're at it, we may as well look at the collapse of Communism in the Eastern Bloc as well:

Five Reasons Why the Eastern Bloc Fragmented

1. The development of nuclear weapons west of the division, and thus the rising possibility that a war might result in apocalyptic outcomes, preventing the socialist states from military advancement.

2. The general lack of evidence pointing to an improvement in the economic circumstances within the Communist world, causing a lack of faith and enthusiasm for Communist lifestyle and the idea of reaching 'true Communism'.

3. The decline of ideological stability among the populace as what have been recognised as capitalist principles, e.g. corruption and inequality, became apparent in Communist regimes.

4. The development of western capitalism to a stage regarded as acceptable by many of the would-be exploited in the west, internally strengthening capitalist society and removing the strong base of proletarian support the socialist states could have relied upon for revolution, or at least sympathy, within these countries.

5. The struggle for the stagnating autocratic regimes to maintain power over the populations of Eastern Europe and the Soviet Union in the face of modernisation, coupled with the weakening of their authority in general.

I'll finish with this thought: Tito is long dead, and Yugoslavia dissolved over two decades ago. Yet if this hadn't happened, that is to say, if the political climate had been such that the new state was able to emerge, who knows what the result would have been. Perhaps the proletariat of these nations would have lined up under Tito's leadership, against the troops of the USA, the USSR, Great Britain, the People's Republic of Poland, France and Hungary; perhaps the task of revolution would have entailed a struggle against not only the capitalist, but also the Communist world.

It's ironic, when you think about it, and fairly shameful for both sides of the Berlin Wall. Just imagine how Stalin, the man who is quoted to have said 'I will shake my little finger and there will be no more Tito!' would have reacted.

13. THE PULL OF THE CENTRE

Posted on April 10, 2015

As all the voters in the UK will know, May the 7th is approaching and tensions are running high. The first TV debate between party leaders has been aired, the first signs of future change on ground level are appearing, and policy announcements are growing even more forceful, more desperate, as the day nears.

Of course, I'm talking about the British general election, but I'm not about to take a side. Rather, I'm writing to talk about the turning point this election presents, and what it could mean for the future of British politics. Specifically, I want to address the question brought forward by the establishment of the current coalition government: is traditional Left/Right politics in Britain on the decline?

One thing is becoming increasingly clear: the coalition established after 2010's vote was cast is the first to have been in power since 1945, yet it seems unlikely that it will be the last. The usual distinctions between a Labour and a Conservative voter are wearing away rapidly, possibly along with the obvious social distinctions that once separated the two groups, and it now seems inconceivable that the population could be divided into the supportive constituencies that these two parties once laid claim to. Really, if we look at it from this angle, it doesn't seem surprising that nobody in 2010 could secure an outright majority, and it suggests that nobody will

this year either, but what does this say about the future of party democracy?

The latter half of the previous century has seen, among many other phenomena, party politics drift slowly towards the centre; once in a position where they could be viewed as the country's answer to the radical European workers' movements on the eve of the Russian Revolution, the Labour Party has grown so moderate in its approach that it could be seen to have rejected socialism entirely; once truly conservative, the Conservative Party recently legalised homosexual marriage, straying far from what once were its core, underlying values of tradition and, well, conservatism. Assuming such a trend continues, we can logically predict a point in the near future where the current necessity of a party to vote for is no longer apparent, where Left/Right politics o longer exists. So, to answer the question, I believe that the political divide in Britain is, in fact, on the decline, and has been for some time.

I understand that this view seems contradicted by the increase in popularity of smaller parties (the Green Party or the United Kingdom Independence Party (UKIP) providing examples in Britain's case), which are often more firmly rooted in the philosophies that once drove the Labour or Conservative parties. I wouldn't see this as a contradiction to my view, rather a side effect of the model that it proposes. In other words, I believe it's natural that as the mainstream parties lose their ideological ground, vast territories in the Left and Right are left unoccupied, which other movements will rise to claim. I don't, however, believe that the cycle will repeat, that UKIP will become the 'new Conservatives', and I think the fact that no serious movement on the Left or Right has arisen proves this; all we are seeing is splinter factions take a temporary stand as the original political ties fragment, as the original divisions crumble, but they too will either move towards the centre or be reduced to insignificance.

On that note, if such a trend represents the political situation of western democracy as a whole, rather than just a one-time occurrence in Britain, then the UK as a country is by no means at the forefront of this change. Europe, for example, is a continent used to the rule of coalition governments, even those which constitute polar opposites. Just look at Greece, in which the latest general election brought to power a coalition between a radical leftist, neo-Communist party and a centre-Right movement, linked only by their opposition to austerity imposed by the EU.

So, if such change is occurring worldwide, and democracy is slowly becoming a battle between individuals rather than ideologies, then what can be done about it? Should we resist the change? Should we back the smaller, radically orientated parties just to repel the pull of the centre? I suppose it's up to you, but the way I see it, there's not a lot we can do to change things. I believe that, like the issues caused by voting inequality roughly a century ago, we'll get over this one by confronting it head-on.

Of course, I may be entirely deluded, in which case there's nothing to worry about, and even if I'm right, it can't be all bad news; it may even be refreshing for people to break the ties they once had with their parties. After all, this needn't be viewed as the end of one political era. Rather, you could see it as the start of the next.

Either way, keep voting and we'll soon see what happens!

Russ and Oli on October 18, 2015 at 8:04 pm said:

Great article.... This one is a bit like the ice cream sellers on a beach. The only logical place for the first one is in the centre of the beach which allows them to maximise trade. Where should the second one go? Where should the other one go if one moves to left or right? This was the prevailing orthodoxy for Blair/Clinton years I believe.

Does it still apply? Well the Tories moved left (at least in rhetoric if not in deed) at their last party conference...

14. ON PATRIOTISM

Posted on April 18, 2015

As I write, patriotic thought is on the rise.

From the nationalist, anti-US current developing in Russia to the successes of far-Right parties across the UK with the increase in foreign immigration, the country one belongs to surfaces more and more when discussing politics. This is probably due to a variety of factors, perhaps as a reaction against the political and economic unions of today, such as the EU, or in the form of national self-determination, opposing the rule of other nations, such as in Scotland or Kashmir. It would thus seem wrong to make assumptions or generalisations regarding such a vague and simple manner of political thought, though there is an underlying definition to be understood.

If you simply type in the word 'patriotism', here's what Google will give you:

patriotism
/'peɪtrɪətɪz(ə)m/
Noun
the quality of being patriotic; vigorous support for one's country.
'a highly decorated officer of unquestionable integrity and patriotism'

In the entry 'Nationalism, Imperialism and Communism' I made clear my hatred for nationalism. Today, against the backdrop of an increasingly patriotic world, I'll take that one step further and explain why I believe patriotic thought, even in casual circumstances, is unhealthy, damaging and also completely irrational.

Take Russia, for example, a country in which 'vigorous support for one's country' is actually able to translate itself into 'hatred of another'. Is this not proof that patriotism is a corrupting manner of thought; one that is able to completely distort perceptions of the world? Any leader could cultivate such a force, using it to brainwash their population and justify inhumane actions 'for the glory of the motherland'. Patriotism, capable of arising in any country under any regime, can counteract the process of fair, logical decision-making, when an individual will side with their country no matter what. Even 'weaker' patriots, happy to draw limits on their support for the nation, fall into the same trap: if you belong to a country, if you *believe* in that country, then imagine how readily biased you'd be in the need to choose a side.

This can be clearly seen in the example of the Vietnam War, in which many atrocities, violations of international treaties and inhumane acts of violence were committed by the United States in the invasion of an innocent country thousands of miles away. This war in particular drew a great deal of internal opposition, yet a proportion of society managed to be persuaded, and that was enough. If these people had been born without a nationality, without any reason to side with the US government, I'm certain that fewer would have chosen to do so. Thus, many that could prevent authorities from committing such atrocities do not, merely because they blindly support the country of their birth, for no real reason whatsoever.

Yet this isn't even the worst of it; to develop a true understanding of this idea, I believe it's necessary to consult history, and what does this tell us?

Well, as you might have expected, it's not good news...

The twentieth century saw the establishment of patriotism in its most extreme format, with the global rise of fascism. A fascist regime is an example of patriotism taken to the furthest extent possible, with nationalistic thought not only embedded in the regime, but existing as the basis upon which the government, the military and the economy all stand. The ideas that motivated Hitler, Mussolini or Franco were not only patriotic in nature; they also placed the idea of national glory where the Communists of the day placed the achievement of a classless society. In other words, they valued their nation more than anything.

To reach conclusions, however, we must look at the regimes from which these move-
ments arose, for a trend in fascist nations such as the Third Reich, Mussolini's Italy or Imperial Japan is clearly visable: each one of them quite simply formed out of a miserable society. This could have been due to a disaster, such as the horrific earthquake in Japan in the 1920s, which is thought to have sparked the

rise of Japanese imperialism, or just a general desire for change, such as in post-1918 Germany. Either way (doubtless, there are also many other ways), we can see a trend developing here. Nationalism, like a political tumour, has a tendancy to arise out of chaos. It ties the people of a nation together using an already existing middle ground, and gives them something to believe in when nothing else does. It isn't surprising then, that Germany and Italy (two nations where nationalism burned as brightly as ever) were countries in which a revolution was most expected. Instead of staging one, however, the people resorted to an easier form of change, looking to nationalism as a 'cheap' alternative.

Whilst these three countries are obviously extreme examples, they reveal a great deal about patriotism in general. The idea develops as a creed that the populace will turn to when they have nothing left to believe in; they chose to place their faith in the most simple idea available, this being their own country. It has the potential to curb real political change and distracts the population from the truth of the matter, however appalling that truth may be. Just look at the military, who often endure horrific conditions whilst living in fear of their lives, and desperately need something to believe in, something to fight for, something which enables them to keep pushing on. It's no surprise that patriotism is not only rife among the fighting forces but is also implemented artificially by those in command.

I think I've made clear why such thought is far from healthy and should be considered dangerous, but I'd like to finish by pointing out what it really means, and why this is relevant in discussing the concept.

What does it mean to be a patriot?

As a simple definition of the term, the one given above is adequate, yet what 'vigorous support for one's country' actually consists of is an entirely different matter.

I'd consider it vital to understand that 'one's country' consists of no more than several hundred square kilometres inside an artificially drawn borderline, somewhere in which one live one's life. It may sound like a romantic idea, yet it's actually plainly ridiculous, despite how many continue to cling to it.

On that note, coming back to the UK, several informative UKIP leaflets recently came through my door in the run-up to the general election. Reading through what the party had to say, I noticed that the slogan 'Believe in Britain' was used (well, in fact it was proudly displayed in capitals).

'Why?' I found myself asking. 'What is there to believe in about Britain? In itself, the UK is merely a relatively small nation-state off the north-western coast of Europe. Within this country there are many greats, yet there are also many wrongdoers, and I'm not too sure what makes the general spread of the population so special. Perhaps you should tell me to 'Believe in UKIP', but what is there to glorify about one country out of hundreds, which just so happens to be the one in which I live and which you intend to govern?'

It certainly seems odd. Surely we're too intelligent to devote ourselves entirely to an area of land, simply because it was the one we grew up in, or live in today.

Sadly though, this just isn't true.

15. NORTH KOREA: THE BEGINNING OF THE END

Posted on April 24, 2015

In the preface to *Communism: A Very Short Introduction*, Leslie Holmes writes:

> '*The overwhelming majority of states that were Communist as recently as the late 1980s have moved on. While, formerly, five Communist states remain, the two successful ones (China and Vietnam) are so largely because they have jettisoned many of the original basic tenants of Communism and are in some important areas – notably the economy – already post-Communist.*'

The Communist world today

First published in 2009, this view is already proving to be especially discerning. Only in late 2014 did the USA and Cuba set aside their long-enduring hostility towards one another, an action which, as I've earlier said, I believe will mark the start of socialism's decline in the Caribbean.

Arguably, with China and Vietnam already long gone, this leaves just one state that exists according to strictly socialist principles: North Korea, or officially the Democratic People's Republic of Korea (DPRK).

Ironically, what could be perceived to be the last untarnished Communist regime has formally abandoned Communist philosophy, a political step on the road to capitalism which the other four countries have yet to take, with its constitution of 2009 describing the country as one 'guided in its activities by the Juche idea and the Songun idea'. However, Juche, the school of thought based upon ideas of self-sufficiency, and Songun, the national policy of 'military first', so little to alter the country's strictly centralised economy. From the outside, it would appear that the economic situation has persisted without interruption, leaving a country with a system that is as 'Communistic' system as the other four – even more so today, with the relaxations in policy within China and Vietnam. But is all this about to change?

A surprising event in recent news may indicate exactly that, depending on the angle from which you look at it; North Korea is currently experiencing a nationwide property boom, a concept we'd associate with the capitalist west. In itself, this may not provide a strong enough argument to suggest a foreshadowing of the regime's collapse, but an article published in the South Korean newspaper the *Hankyoreh* explains how this may be the case. The author references research professor Jung Eun-yi, a leading expert in the field, who 'argues that there are signs that the housing market in North Korea is turning into a real estate market, rather like South Korea'.

As I've said, it's still only a minor alteration, yet change has to begin somewhere, and it isn't always as dramatic as the Romanian Revolution of 1989, or even the lifting of the trade embargo against Cuba by the USA. Furthermore, it shouldn't be underestimated how provocative such a change could be; the article explains how Jung believes this style of market 'will continue to expand for a significant period of time', allowing it to seriously transform the nationwide economy, and paving the way for further relaxations on the road to a free market. In short, we learn that Jung thinks the establishment of the housing delegation offices in 2013 proves that 'both central planning and market forces are at work in the North Korean economy today', and that, in her opinion, the incorporation of the latter alongside the former into the market also provides evidence for a reformist trend developing under Kim Jong-un's government; she informs us that 'the regime is going beyond the military-first policy known as *Songun* that was instituted by Kim's father and moving down the path toward socialist capitalism'.

The timing certainly seems right, with the DPRK standing as the last of its kind, and I believe this is exactly the kind of trigger such transition requires. Once more opportunities arise for personal financial gain, enabling the individual, rather than the state, to profit, the iron grip the government maintains the economy will begin to loosen; like the other socialist states whose colours have somehow clung to the mast after the dissolution of the Soviet Union and the fall of the Berlin Wall, the DPRK's regime will eventually crumble. One question, however, remains unanswered: is the fall of Korean Communism to be celebrated or lamented?

There's obviously no one answer, and it depends not only on your attitude towards Communism on the whole, but also towards the North Korean regime. I can't imagine many conservatives, liberals, or even socialists would be saddened at the prospect. A dispute could arise among the far Left, however, and the Communist perspective on North Korea is not uniform.

Personally, I'd definitely support the ousting of the current regime, which operates as an absolute monarchy, enjoys luxurious privileges unheard of by the workers it claims to represent, looks to the leader like a prophet, Kim Il-sung like a god, and all in a perverted fashion which contradicts multiple tenants of Marxism. As for the loss of a Communist system in the economic sense, I feel much the same as I did for the potential loss of Cuba's. Yet it doesn't take an expert to realise that the North Korean system is already flawed, given the famines, the corruption it's tainted by, and the seemingly endless funding it directs towards the military at the expense of the populace. In fact, if you take all its flaws into consideration, it would even seem sensible to argue that North Korea's economy has already strayed too far from the Communist model it was built upon.

16. THE LOST WORLD OF COMMUNIST AFRICA

Posted on May 2, 2015

The very notion of Communism conjures up images of the Siberian tundra, the Berlin Wall, the Moscow skyline, perhaps, against the background of the Soviet flag; images of interpretations in Europe and Asia. Obviously, smaller states exist in the collective memory, probably helped by events such as the Cuban Missile Crisis or the Vietnam War, but there is one area of the world easy to miss: Africa.

What you may not realise is that, whilst as a continent, post-colonial Africa was not allied with any power-block in the way that Eastern or Western Europe was, it was nonetheless home to multiple Communists and Communist regimes, from Ethiopia to Angola. Stories that tend to accompany Communist history, of heroes, of struggle, yet also of terror and coercion, all exist within the continent. However, in the grand scheme of things, the African reds seem to have been largely ignored.

This may be due to the fact that Communism was perhaps not a truly established movement in Africa, rather a reaction to colonialism, and a manner of political thought that resulted from an alliance with the Eastern Block and a need to take a side during the Cold War. Additionally, the fact that comparatively few Communist states existed in the world's second-largest continent has undoubtedly contributed, alongside the actuality that none of them have made a significant appearance on the international stage in the way that Cuba or Vietnam have.

Nonetheless, we certainly can't ignore the millions of lives changed by the regimes established in the region, nor can we forget the dedicated Marxists among the African nationalists and anti-colonialists who fought for the sake of proletarian justice from the start. This is the reason why I've decided to write about the movement, but mainly the people who comprised this movement, of proletarian struggle across the continent.

Here is a brief insight into the lives and achievements of three African revolutionaries, each of whom, for better or for worse, transformed their country dramatically.

Thomas Sankara

Leader of Burkina Faso from 1983 to 1987, Thomas Isidore Noël Sankara was a dedicated Marxist and an advocate of Pan-Africanism. Sankara rose to the position of president on the 4th August 1983, after a successful coup d'état, and led the country until his assassination after a counter-revolutionary insurgency. Although he was only in power for four years, he installed many progressive policies, to combat pressing economic, and social issues which still stand today.

Though Sankara's family wanted him to become a Catholic priest, he embarked on a career in the military from the age of nineteen, before fighting in a border war between Mali and Upper Volta (Burkina Faso). Shortly after, he rose to the position of commander, at which point he met Blaise Compaoré in Morocco. Along with several other officers, Sankara and Compaoré formed the secret organisation known as the *Communist Officers Group*. It could be argued that his Communist associations were a result of the uprisings and the populist movement he had witnessed while training for service in Madagascar.

Sankara first served as secretary of state for information in the country's military government, and later as prime minister, under new leadership brought to power by an insurgency. He was later dismissed, however, and lived under house arrest after what 'Thomas Sankara Website' states was a 'visit by the French president's son and African affairs adviser Jean-Christophe Mitterrand'. His arrest, and that of other officials, sparked a popular revolt. It is thus understandable why the insurgency that brought him to power that August was conducted.

As president, Sankara did much for the benefit of the country, waging a determined struggle against corruption (he changed the country's name from Upper Volta to Burkina Faso, which means 'Land of Incorruptible People'), promoting women's rights and prioritising health and education. Influenced by Fidel Castro, he viewed himself as a true revolutionary, and clear associations can be drawn between his policies and that of other Marxist leaders, such as his establishment of the Committees for the Defence of the Revolution. Thomas Sankara was assassinated in 1987 in the aftermath of the coup which robbed him of his power, but nonetheless remains an iconic figure in the country's history, and the history of Marxism as a whole.

Mengistu Haile Mariam

Like Sankara, Mengistu served as an officer before taking power, participating in a military junta against Ethiopia's emperor, Haile Selassie. He was, apparently, relatively obscure when he and his fellow comrades seized power in the nation, forming the Dergue regime, one of military rule orientated towards Communism.

Three years later, after a power struggle, Mengistu not only rose to significance but took control of the Dergue. From that moment on, his true mercilessness was unveiled in his policies, which showed no compromise to those who opposed him. He once had an officer shot simply because he expressed a desire to make peace with the small, independence-seeking province of Eritrea. Mengistu also embarked on a programme known as the Red Terror, which, according to the leader's profile on the BBC News website: 'killed thousands of intellectuals, professionals, and other perceived opponents of socialism'.

Maintaining an ambition to transform the country into a Communist state orientated towards Stalinism, he developed an alliance with the USSR. In Ethiopia's war with Somalia, the Soviet Union, Cuba and East Germany each assisted the country, leading to its military victory. Military support aside, however, Mengistu apparently relied on the Soviet Union to drive Ethiopia's economy for some time, and it is certainly questionable how long his regime would have survived without the support of others.

In 1991 (also the year in which the USSR collapsed) oppositional military forces advanced on the capital, Addis Ababa, and Mengistu fled the country alongside other officials and family members, finding asylum in Zimbabwe. Despite being charged by the Ethiopian government with killing almost 2,000 individuals, he still lives in what are believed to be luxurious cirumstances today. Ethopia demands his extradition, but Zimbabwe, under Robert Mugabe (a similar character), won't cooperate.

Nelson Mandela?

Is it surprising to see Mandela's name on this list? I was certainly surprised when I first heard of his Communist associations. I question-marked his name as I wasn't quite sure (it's very difficult to be 'quite sure'), but there is certainly sufficient evidence to suggest that Mandela was not just a freedom fighter against the Apartheid regime, but also an advocate of a socialist South Africa.

As a member of the ANC, Mandela, like the rest of the movement, allied himself with the Communists in the country during the Apartheid regime. Though this, in itself, doesn't necessarily expose any tendencies within the ANC, there seems to be greater evidence at hand suggesting the organisation actually contained Communist elements, and thus that such an alliance may, at times, have been more than simply a desire from both sides to unite against a common enemy. An article by Bill Keller in the *Sunday Review* explains this:

'Communist ideology undoubtedly seeped into the ANC, where it became part of a uniquely South African cocktail with African nationalism, black consciousness, religious liberalism and other, inchoate angers and resentments and yearnings.'

In relation to Mandela himself, it is worth noting that he was a member of the South African Communist Party. Alex Newman's article in the World News section of the *New American* states that the party admitted the freedom fighter's role, referring to him as 'Comrade' Mandela. This may not necessarily prove the point conclusively (Bill Keller explained in a previous article that his membership of the party and affiliation with radical Communists 'say less about his ideology than about his pragmatism'), but it does suggest that there is more to the man, who is regarded as a hero throughout the capitalist west, than meets the eye.

'I have cherished the idea of a democratic and free society in which all persons live together in harmony and with equal opportunities'

Nelson Mandela

WEEKLY ENTRIES WILL CEASE TEMPORARILY

Posted on May 8, 2015

Due to work-related issues, I will not be posting on 'The Anonymous Revolutionary' for another few weeks, though entries will continue on Friday June 12.

Thank you for taking notice.

– T.A.R.

17. MARXISM IS A SCIENCE, NOT A RELIGION

Posted on June 12, 2015

As promised, entries resume today, making it an appropriate time to address one thing that's been on my mind in the weeks after my last post...

Despite the differences in opinion among Communist circles, there are really only two variants of Communist.

Some, I've noticed, manage to incorporate Marxism into their lives as a viewpoint, a belief, and nothing more. The orchestrators of the Russian October Revolution, namely Lenin and Trotsky, are good examples; they acted, commanded, spoke and wrote using Marxism as a tool, a guidance, and a scientific philosophy on the basis of which they would carry out their principles.

Others, just as knowledgeable in Marxism, and just as eager to apply it, look at the philosophy from a different stance. They treat Communist theory as if it were the words of a prophet, and look to Marx, Lenin or Stalin as if they themselves were the divine preachers of such theoretical wisdom. Their great appreciation of socialist ideas trans-forms itself into a cult-like and almost religious worship of socialism, to such an extent that they begin to forget the central tenets and ideas of their philosophy.

As you might imagine, this presents a series of problems...

First of all, this tendency to glorify Communism actually contradicts it. Where it clashes with Marxist theory is not obvious, but we must remember that Marxism, whether correct or not, is a theory of science. It exists based on the idea that the development of society runs parallel to the development of the natural world, applauds rational and scientific thought, and is hardly compatible with the backward, illogical and religious adherence to ideology exemplified by many of its followers (Marx famously referred to religion as 'opium for the masses'). Ask yourself this: in terms of this spiritual 'opium', where does Christianity differ from Marxism-Leninism? When both are treated as religious doctrines, it doesn't.

An extreme example of the blurring between Marxism and religion is that of Stalinist Russia, in which the Communist Party was practically allowed to replace the Orthodox Church. 'Lenin is with us, always' was a phrase popularised under Stalin, who seemed not to let it trouble him that he was cultivating belief of a spiritual nature akin to the religions he was trying to suppress. Other examples can probably be found throughout history, but I hope (for any Stalinists/ Stalin sympathisers reading) it does the job of highlighting just how irrational such regimes can become. Lenin was a great leader and a great theorist, but he wasn't Jesus. Marx, Lenin, Mao and Stalin: they're human beings, not deities, and perhaps we'll remember these people for their contributions to the socialist movement, but to look upon them as divine and holy beings is beyond ridiculous.

In addition to this, I'd like to point out that many in this category, which often tends to be the Stalinists and Maoists of this world (I've noticed that Communist philosophies to the left of Marxism-Leninism don't tend to adopt such views), are highly illogical in their assessment of society, and especially of the Communist world. In this respect, what I was talking about (the almost holy glorification of both the theory and its practitioners), can lead to further problems; if you look to Stalin, Mao or Kim Il-sung the way a religious believer may look to God, it's not surprising that to you, these individuals must be heroes, and thus you'll go to extreme measures to ensure they are treated as such. At the same time, one may go to ridiculous extents to prove their theories or writings are true to the word, immune from the possibility of even minor falsification, as certain Christians may claim about the Bible. This is, of course, just as irrational.

'Nope. Definitely not a Gulag. Can I get away with blaming this on western imperialism? Probably...'

Yet equally bizarre is the manner in which these people try to prove such things are true, or simply justify their beliefs: a favourite technique, and one that is not criticised nearly enough, is historical denial. Just look at the number of leftists who deny Stalin's crimes, who claim that the repression which exists in the DPRK is merely a conspiracy cooked up by imperialist western media. A surprising number of people end up falling into such a trap, to the point where they distort the whole of history to support their beliefs.

Is this Marxian? Is this the kind of mentality you'd expect from those who uphold a view which thrives off the analysis of class history? It's well known, even outside of Communism, that the philosophy relies on the observation of historical patterns. It's thus obvious that anyone distorting history in this way, altering the past to suit their ideals, is transforming events which could prove vital in understanding society from a Marxist perspective. In other words, these people, who tightly cling to Communism as an ideology rather than a philosophy, actually demonstrate an ignorance and a betrayal of Marxist principles whilst attempting to defend views which they believe to be Marxian. What's worse is that, on the whole, I don't believe these people know they're altering history. They *believe* the atrocities we hear of are a concoction of lies drip-fed to the population by the government, and this is a dangerous thing. Certain stories are undoubtedly twisted, and some, if not all, are obviously biased, but we can't escape historical truth, and Communists, perhaps more than anyone, should accept this.

So, if this is the case, then what can be done about it? What is to be done (Leninist reference intended) about the fact that a great proportion of Marxists globally have managed to turn the theory on its head and produce something of an embarrassment to the traditional principles of Communism? Sadly, I don't feel there's a lot that *can* be done. We just have to accept that a great deal of the world, including the former Communist world, lives (or lived) according to these strange and perverse views. Nonetheless, I urge any leftists out there not to let themselves be absorbed into this twisted form of socialism, and as for those who glorify Mao or Stalin (or, for that matter, Marx or Engels), who look to their works as if to a holy scripture, and who consider themselves the rightful heirs of 'Mao Tse-tung thought' or whatever other titles they grant themselves, I encourage you, quite frankly, to wake up from this delusional dream.

18. ON VISITING MOSCOW

Posted on June 27, 2015

First of all, I'll apologise for not posting last week; I was in Russia from Thursday to Sunday, and didn't have enough time between sightseeing to post anything worth reading. However, I saw a great deal when I otherwise would have written something, and I thought I'd dedicate this entry to the places I've been and the observations I made on the trip.

This entry will basically be a range of different photographs I took around the city (may be more of a photo album than anything else, but I have to do something with these images!), to give you a flavour of what the country looks like today. Bear in mind that I only saw Moscow, and other parts of Russia will be undoubtedly very different, although nevertheless, seeing the city in the flesh told me a great deal about the nation; not only was the experience very interesting, but it shed light on multiple attitudes and stereotypes I'd come to adopt about the place.

So here is a short history of my time in the Russian Federation...

After arriving in Domodedovo airport, I stayed here, in the Moscow Leningradskaya hotel. Now owned by Hilton, it was originally built by Stalin as one of the leader's 'Seven Sisters' (seven towers to decorate the Moscow skyline).

As you step out of the hotel, you're greeted by several railway stations built to connect different faraway locations, such as Belarus or the city of Saint Petersburg. Here are a few shots of these stations, each of them grand and significant.

One thing you quickly notice is the casual presence of Communist imagery, which nobody has removed since the dissolution of the Soviet Union. Small architectural details on these buildings, dating back to the Soviet times, suggest that the USSR has not vanished entirely. Perhaps the 'spectre of Communism', which overthrew the tsar and built the world's first socialist state, has not quite departed Russia...

...on the other hand, perhaps it has:

Another aspect of the city which I found astonishing was its series of underground railway stations, which were also constructed when Moscow served as the Soviet capital. In the 1930s, rather than building an average underground rail system, Stalin decided to build a network of 'palaces for the people', and constructed an array of subterranean estates of granite and red marble. Thanks to Koba's project, Moscow now has a fantastic metro!

Here, statues of both soldiers and civilians litter the station. Regarding the statue portrayed, it is considered good luck to touch the dog's nose (a ritual which students are known to practise before exams, apparently).

The ghost of Lenin still haunts the Moscow underground.

**"For Lenin, the teachings
of Marx were right
because they were true."**

Marshal Zukov guards the gates of Red Square with a hand gesture that appears somewhat repressive, but apparently is just culturally Russian (you'll see the same gesture made by the statue of the soldier if you ever visit the Soviet War Memorial in Berlin).

If you look closely, you'll see that the horse is actually stamping on the Swastika with its bizarrely straight front legs.

The red star below stands over the Kremlin Wall's Spasskaya Tower.

Above is one of the two variations on the sign of the cross that I noticed in the country. Apparently, the slanting bar represents a ladder (the idea that one may step up to heaven or down to hell), and the additional oblong is representative of the original cross, which allegedly featured a plaque marked 'Son of God'.

Here's the other variation, featuring the crescent. The unofficial explanation for its presence is that the moon beneath the cross symbolises victory over Islam, but the real one is that the moon is in fact not a moon at all, but a boat, representing the arc.

The frontier of GUM, Moscow's leading department store:

Finally, I give you the street outside the Bolshoi Theatre, under a downpour. This is almost definitely the wrong time of day for the rain qualify as such, but I learnt an interesting Russian expression whilst walking through the rain in Moscow: when it rains whilst the sun is shining, it is referred to as 'mushroom rain', because these are apparently the optimal conditions for growing mushrooms in the forest.

If I was to summarise my trip, I could draw several conclusions from it. As I said previously, it certainly changed my attitude towards the country and the culture, as well as the previous ideas I had about the city. Before visiting, for example, I expected a somewhat cold and soulless city. I anticipated a very interesting journey, and hoped to see fascinating, but perhaps not beautiful sights, based on everything I'd heard about Russia. After seeing the place, however, my opinions have changed completely; I was struck by how modern, how stylish, and also how gentle the city was. With the wide streets, leafy parks and a surprisingly quiet and empty city centre, you could be in Prague or Paris. To put it into context, I visited Berlin last summer for a similar kind of holiday, which felt colder, and, in a way, harsher than Moscow did. Out of the two, I felt that Moscow was the prettier city.

Another aspect of Russia which I had braced myself for was the stereotype of unfriendliness sometimes associated with Russian culture, but I certainly didn't find there to be any truth behind such a view. In fact, everyone I met seemed polite and happy to help, and it actually proved relatively easy to buy tickets or order food through interacting with the locals, despite the obvious language barriers. Unless my experience was an entirely unique one, I can tell you that such a stereotype is incorrect, and that life as a tourist isn't nearly as hard as it's made out to be. Just remember to count the number of stops on the Metro, because, if you can't speak Russian, you're likely to forget the name of your station!

To cut a long story short, these two days have been fantastic, and to any potential travellers, all I can say about the city is positive. I hope to return some day, and would definitely recommend visiting.

До Свидания

— T.A.R.

Marta Frant on June 28, 2015 at 7:04 am said:

I was surprised by the fact that you anticipated seeing a 'soulless city'. Russians consider themselves as a very 'soulful' (душевная) nation. To me, people in St. Petersburg are even friendlier than people from Moscow.

By the way I'm glad you enjoyed visiting our capital :)

19. THE EVOLUTION OF COMMUNIST SYMBOLISM

Posted on July 3, 2015

From left to right: the emblem used by the Communist Party of Britain; the Communist Party USA's logo; ...and finally, the Communist Party of Ireland's flag

Above are three examples of the way in which Communist imagery is used today, showing how some traditional symbols – the hammer and sickle, for instance – have been adapted to represent further ideas (as in the Communist Party of Britain's emblem, in which the dove symbolises peace), or perhaps simply for artistic individuality (as would appear to be the case in the Communist Party USA's logo).

Yet whist considerably different from Communist imagery used sixty, seventy or eighty years ago, similar symbols are portrayed. The colour red, the hammer and sickle, and, though not actually portrayed in the images above, the Communist star, have certainly survived the test of time as the international symbols of radical socialism, which is inter-esting, since many of the ideas behind such imagery relate more closely to the conditions where they developed than they do to Communism itself. The hammer and sickle, for example, developed in revolutionary Russia to represent a union between the Russian peasantry and the industrial proletariat, and whilst the colour red did have an association with revolutionary leftism in Europe prior to 1917, it is also deeply associated with Russian culture (the Russian word for the colour red (красный) is very similar to the word meaning 'beautiful' (красивый). As for the five-pointed star, there are different theories about its origins, with some believing that the five points represent the five continents, and others, that they represent the five groups which would overthrow the Russian tsar, these being the peasantry, the industrial workers, the soldiers, the intelligentsia and the youths.

Either way, we can definitely see a trend developing here; much of what we associate with Communism worldwide is actually more closely associated with an individual country than anything else, relating to specific ideas that would only apply to the USSR. Yet this hasn't stopped the exportation of these ideas internationally, not only among the socialist nations but through Communist parties and movements operating within capitalist countries, from Peru to South Africa. So the question I'll be answering today is this: how have these icons, often specific and relevant only to the revolutionary movement in the Russian Empire, been adapted to the multiple conditions in which they have been used?

Throughout the Twentieth Century...

I'll start with the flag of China, the second country to experience a successful, independent revolution. This flag features one large star in the top left-hand corner, surrounded to the right by four smaller stars against a red background. The stars are yellow and the background is red, both of which are colours used in the Soviet flag, yet if you look carefully, you'll notice that the red background is a lighter shade on the Chinese flag than on that of the Soviet Union.

According to the website World Atlas, the large star represents Communism, whilst the four smaller stars represent the social classes in China. Apparently, the total number of stars (five) 'reflect the importance placed on the number five in Chinese thought and history'.

In this case, the hammer and sickle don't make an appearance, though it is obvious that Communist connotations have been used, with the design creatively blending socialist imagery with features of Chinese society and culture. Such a trend can also be seen in the designs and emblems of both Communist movements and countries of that period...

Here, the flag used by Yugoslavian partisans during World War Two is almost identical to that of the former Yugoslavian kingdom, with the single addition of the red star signifying Communist ideology. Although, like the flag of China, it does seem to combine Marxist and national imagery, it appears to place a heavier emphasis on national, rather than Communist identity. Since the red background is also present on the flag of Albania prior to Communism, the same can be said for that of the Democratic Government of Albania.

We can see from these examples how the revolutionary movement in the twentieth century brought about a whole new wave of art, displaying the merging of political and cultural symbols; the combination of national and international imagery, which can perhaps be seen most clearly in the flags of these revolutionary countries. But, if this was largely the case in the twentieth century, what about the Communist movement in the following one?

After the Fall of Communism...
It's difficult to find political examples of socialist imagery after the dissolution of the Soviet Union and the fall of Communism in Europe, though certain parties and organisations around the world appear to have followed in the same national/Communist trend, such as the Communist Party of Belarus (the logo of which is displayed below showing

the star, the hammer and sickle, and the open book superimposed on the outline of the country) and others (like those displayed at the beginning) have adapted such symbols in their own individual ways.

Other than in these small organisations, however, socialist art hasn't exactly flourished; no new Communist states have arisen, and the now greatly diminished Communist world hasn't made any great cultural contributions since 1991, although one interesting change did occur...

After the end of the Cold War, Communism gradually became less of a threat to the stability of society. As a result, the culture of hatred that developed around the idea began to wear away, and people began to analyse Marxism from a more open, more casual perspective, creating a generation who looked to the Left in what is perhaps a more superficial way.

This gave rise to a bizarre, blatantly ironic, commercial industry, one which I've already mentioned in my entry 'The Commercialisation of Communism', that exploited a range of Communist symbols (often bringing them back from history's grave) for profit-making purposes.

Following On...

When it comes to the future of such art, who knows what will arise (or what won't)? We live among certain symbols and icons which change all the time, like party logos, and some that have stuck around for thousands of years, like the cross of Christianity, and it's interesting to imagine which path Communism will travel down. Assuming some change occurs, one (by this I mean I) could waste hours predicting the symbols and icons that will develop Communist connotations. Quite possibly, in a world where capitalism has undergone significant evolution, the hammer – representing the industrial worker – may no longer be applicable, yet what will replace it is down to the future conditions to follow.

On second thoughts, perhaps we'll stick with the classic imagery of the 1900s, with both movements and countries worldwide reluctant to alter the icons which represent such a great deal of history. After all, there's certainly something unifying about these symbols and the ideas contained within them, and it's hard to imagine that this will be simply forgotten. In the words of John Thune, 'I believe our flag is more than just cloth and ink. It is a universally recognized symbol that stands for liberty, and freedom.' If the Communist movement felt the same about their beloved red banner, perhaps these icons will still be around for hundreds of years.

If change does occur, however, I'm willing to bet that any future development of Communist symbolism will stick to the same theme, this being inequality; I think we'll still see imagery, like the hammer and sickle, that glorifies the exploited class in the current scenario. This might be in the form of an icon representing their suffering or exploitation, or a tool they are associated with, which represents their labour, be it a robot or laser gun (insert any future gadgets or technologies you find to be appropriate here) but given that Communism, by its very nature, emancipates the weak and exploited, I'm certain that it'll be these people who inspire any future art of the revolution.

Either way, I'm looking forward to seeing the result.

20. SUFFERING IN THE FIRST WORLD: GREECE AND THE EUROPEAN CRISIS

Posted on July 11, 2015

To all those out there who follow the Maoist (Third-Worldist) tendency; who uphold the belief that the developed world – Europe, Russia, North America and certain parts of Australasia and East Asia – is a realm of the wealthy, free of any real oppression, this entry is for you.

Very recently, the EU offered a hopeless, desperate Greece its latest proposal for a bailout deal, which, whilst potentially easing the crisis in which the country is currently submerged, would carry strict measures in the way of austerity. The referendum as to whether or not the country should accept called for a rejection, with the population (now largely irritated with the EU and the straining demands they imposed on Greece's already-disastrous economy) probably feeling they'd been down that road before. Yesterday, however, Prime Minister Tsipras announced that Greece would accept the deal regardless, undoubtedly sparking tensions among civilians and party members alike. Whether he had any confidence in the decision or simply yielded to the demands from Brussels we'll never know, but either way, one thing is profoundly clear: the country is truly in dire straits.

There are, however, those who claim otherwise; a significant number entertain the illusion that the developed world, of which Greece is a member, is, by nature, wealthy. They claim that, unlike those in countries like India or Bangladesh, who do experience genuine hardship, the populations of Europe and America lead comparatively luxurious lives. In short, they believe that whilst developing nations do suffer exploitation and poverty, developed countries like Greece know nothing of the sort.

This belief is upheld largely, though not exclusively, by those who adhere to the philosophy of Maoism (Third-Worldism). This particular branch of Maoist Communism believes that capitalist exploitation no longer takes place within the confines of national borders, that the first-world countries have effectively become bourgeois nations which thrive off the exploitation of other, poorer parts of the world. The theory enjoys significant popularity among the Communist movement today, partly because it can explain why the working classes are now shrinking in numbers in the first world but not in the third, and it is, to some degree, accurate. It is obvious, for example, that the first world does profit from the exploitation of the third, with a great deal of our clothes and gadgets now produced overseas, yet the fact that developed economies exploit undeveloped ones is not to say that these economies do not cause suffering at home too; Just look at the poverty experienced by many in Russia, or even America – the heartland of wealth and capital – in which 49 million people, or one in four children (according to the documentary *A Place at the Table*) don't know where their next meal is coming from.

Today, Greece is our example, and the recent crisis in the country can certainly lead to similar horrors to those listed above; I've heard reports of how many have been forced to leave their modernised lives and work the land to survive, whilst the unemployment record in the country reached a record of 28% in November 2013 (to put it into context, the proportion of unemployed Americans during the Great Depression was lower than 25%), and homelessness, once a foreign concept to the Greeks, rocketed. Sadly, the rise in what BBC News describes as the 'New Homeless' coincided with the particularly harsh winter of 2011–12, leaving many exposed to the freezing temperatures with little more than a blanket to protect them from the cold.

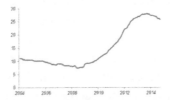

Greek unemployment, 2004–2015

There is, of course, the argument that such hardship is a result of a recession, as opposed to the capitalistic exploitation of the Greek people, and that, whilst capitalism ruins many lives in India or China, it is not responsible for this particular disaster. Yet a similar situation undoubtedly exists among what the advocates of Maoism (Third-Worldism) call the revolutionary proletariat in these aforementioned countries: although not everybody in this part of the world lives under the shackles of First-Worldist exploitation, the poverty experienced by the majority of the population (including these people) is still reflective of the unequal distribution of wealth caused by the former, and thus, the economic system can be held responsible for their

113

impoverishment. The same can be said for the Greek population, as the crisis which ruined these people is rooted directly in the capitalistic economies of Greece and Europe. Therefore capitalism is still the force that reduced them to poverty.

Additionally, I believe that whilst refuting Maoism (Third-Worldism) is important, the crisis also serves a more general purpose in reminding us of just how vulnerable we, the capitalist world, actually are. It would be easy to assume, from the bubble of ignorance provided by a comfortable western lifestyle, that this kind of thing doesn't occur in our neck of the woods; that capitalism today cannot bring about such misery. It's important to avoid falling into this trap, for such a crisis could happen where you live too. If nothing else, treat the event as a news story, one informing the planet that misery and suffering do, and will continue, to exist in the first world.

21. THE BIRTH AND DEVELOPMENT OF CAPITALISM

Posted on July 17, 2015

On Tuesday 14th, many undoubtedly celebrated Bastille Day, paying respect to the rebel movement behind the French Revolution.

Probably the most significant event in eighteenth-century Europe, this revolution reshaped European history, changing the face of France for ever. For anyone unaware of what actually occurred during these remarkable few years, violence broke out across the nation after the Bastille was stormed by revolutionary forces. The rebels would later overthrow the monarchy, and the country would be thrown into chaos triggering a series of conflicts extending as far as the Middle East. These events would be secured in the minds of many generations to come. Even with these drastic outcomes aside, it still deserves a place in world history, for this was the event that brought about an economic system still standing today; this was the event that brought about capitalism.

The idea of a capitalist revolution may sound foreign to you, which is understandable; in a world where capitalism has long been the system that nations have tried to prevent from overthrow by revolution, the thought that it could exist as a revolutionary theory may sound strange to many, yet just like Communism, capitalism had to start somewhere, and 1793 is one of the strongest examples. If the transition it enacted isn't obvious, we have to remember that feudalism – the system's predecessor – was the era of landlords, peasants, absolute monarchy and a heavy religious influence on the populace. All of the above were revoked or transformed after the transfer of power took place, and the main focus of production was no longer the peasants labouring on the aristocrats' land, but the workforce in the factories of Paris, Lyon and Toulouse.

Bataille de Jemmapes, 1792

However, although possibly the most dramatic, the transition in France is obviously not the only example; it is believed by many that capitalism originated many years ago, in the regions of northern Italy, and the ideas of a revolution against feudalism can be seen in the English Civil War, the European Enlightenment, and events reaching as far back as the Crisis of the Late Middle Ages. To give you an idea of how long unrest had been present, Europe – arguably the most advanced continent at that time – experienced almost half a millennium of tensions and trauma with the rise of the new productive means. As a result, society saw many profound changes up to the late eighteenth century, at which point France had finally reformed its economy.

But we have to remember that at this stage, many nations were still stuck in the dark ages of serfdom, and though they would later progress, they did so in a different manner. In the podcast 'Is Marxism a Science?' provided by wearemany. org, the speaker David Whitehouse discusses this when he refers to the German transition to capitalism, which, whilst revolutionary in its own way, was not dramatic or profound like that in France. The states of Germany, as Whitehouse explains, were yet to catch up with more advanced European nations, and thus constructed industrialised economies whilst still under feudal leadership. The same can be said for the third world, which were still not completely capitalistic, but relied on this kind of 'uneven development' (as he puts it) to allow progression to occur.

Carl Stilling: *The Forge* – Germany, 1909

We can also see how such development has possibly occurred on a deeper level in countries like Russia or, perhaps more profoundly, China, for these were largely feudal and backward regimes, yet in both, Communist revolutions (or, at least, revolutions claiming to be of a Communist nature) took place. Here it would appear that not only has development occurred on an uneven level, with both feudal and capitalistic features present, but it has almost completely skipped a stage. Whether or not these revolutions were truly Marxist is a debate for another time, but the preface to the Communist Manifesto's Russian edition talks of the peasantry possibly building Communism in the country, suggesting that such a progression may be possible, and thus that capitalism need not always develop fully.

Even if this isn't the case, we can see through this pattern of mixed progress – where undeveloped societies were forced to prematurely catch up with developed ones – the extent to which capitalism has transformed the world through its own evolution; Western Europe and North America have practically raced ahead, forcing other regions of the world to industrialise quickly, and this is all down to the colossal scale on which capitalist production took place. On this subject, Marx also wrote that the bourgeois class, 'during its rule of scarcely 100 years has created more massive and more colossal productive forces than have all preceding generations together', which allows us to see how the implementation and the spread of capitalism has truly revolutionised society.

22. ON TROTSKYISM

Posted on July 25, 2015

What is Trotskyism?

Unlike specific doctrines or philosophies such as Leninism, or perhaps Marxism in general, Trotskyism has no one definition – it is simply a collection of the ideas and theories put forward by Leon Trotsky. However, whilst perhaps not as easy to summarise as the ideas of Marx and Lenin, they are by no means insignificant, for Trotsky's followers founded one of the two key movements which worked to redefine twentieth-century Communism; alongside the Stalinist interpretation of Soviet-style Marxism (which later developed into Marxism-Leninism), Trotskyism split Communism in two, forcing Marxists everywhere to take sides.

To give you an idea of what exactly it calls for, here is a brief summary of its ideas and theories:

- A strong adherence to the international revolutionary movement, which fuels the theory of Permanent Revolution (a theoretical argument that states revolution can take place in backward, agrarian countries such as Russia, so long as there is a simultaneous international revolution to strengthen it).
- An encouragement for the involvement of workers in the state system, and the criticism of 'Stalinist' regimes for their excessively bureaucratic and authoritarian interpretation of Communism.

- A general critical attitude towards Stalin's Russia and the Soviet Union after 1924, due to its betrayal of both the aforementioned values.

Recently, I decided that I myself am a Trotskyist, this being the inspiration for today's post. For a long while I'd thought of myself as somewhere to the left of Marxism-Leninism, so I was looking closely at tendencies such as Left Communism, ultra-Leftism and Trotskyism to try and determine which category I fell into, at which point I decided that my views matched Trotsky's ideas more closely than anybody else's. Given that I've written several paragraphs on these ideas, you may wonder why exactly I've chosen to do this, or what relevance they have today that would make writing about them worthwhile. I'll answer this in a short while – first, I think it's important to understand them from a historical perspective, allowing us to comprehend their development in society.

Below is an excerpt from the document 'For Trotskyism!' which can be found on the homepage of the International Bolshevik Tendency, a modern-day Trotskyist organisation, where the movement is described...

It was verified in a positive sense in the October Revolution in 1917, the greatest event in modern history, and generally negatively since. After the bureaucratic strangulation of the Bolshevik Party and the Comintern by the Stalinists, the tradition of Leninism – the practice and program of the Russian Revolution – was carried forward by the Left Opposition and by it alone.

This says it all: Trotskyism has a bad name. Ever since such 'strangulation' the idea had developed taboo connotations, even becoming an insult among Communists. As a result, the number of Trotskyist movements is relatively small, and was probably even smaller in the days of the USSR. Following his departure from Soviet politics, Trotsky was the great outcast, the traitor, the enemy of the Soviet regime, and any of his followers were inevitably handed the same label.

Not surprisingly, then, no socialist states have arisen in accordance with Trotsky's views or theories, and the few who adhere to them have been forced to get their word across through whatever tactics are available, such as electoral participation or entryism (a good example of the latter being Militant, a Trotskyist organisation in Britain working within the Labour Party throughout the 1970s and 80s). In other words, it would appear that Trotskyism, for the most part, died with Leon Trotsky.

The organisation's logo

So, coming back to the question of relevance, it may seem to be the case that these theories, written over seventy years ago and only partially developed since, are far from relevant; one might be inclined to take the view that it was an ideology rooted out of the Communist movement long ago, which has since been rejected worldwide, and even today is still on the side-lines of leftist politics. After all, Stalinism aside, who's to say that there wasn't a rationale behind the rejection of Trotskyism?

I, however, would disagree, and would take the view that time has actually helped prove Trotsky correct, an example of this being the fact that his ideas are centred on a criticism of the Soviet system (or rather the Soviet system as Stalin had modelled it) and thus they deserve at least some credit, purely due to the fact that the Soviet Union collapsed. I'd see it like this: Socialism in One Country, the policy which, originally adopted under Stalin, influenced the country henceforth, halted efforts to spread the revolution beyond national boundaries. Thus the USSR, like its European satellite states, was left with no option but to try and cultivate socialism from within, which led to stagnation, corruption, and ultimately, failure. I believe that this is proof, or at least hard evidence, that Socialism in One Country is impossible, thus making Trotsky's argument especially perceptive.

Obviously, I don't mean to argue that Trotsky's word was entirely unfalsified – that would be counter-scientific and thus contrary to the spirit of Marxism – and he did create work that was proven inaccurate, but I do believe that his ideas and his contributions to Marxist philosophy are worthy of recognition, and, what's more, worthy of consideration today. In a world with no Soviet Union, after the fall of Stalinist Communism, today's Marxists definitely need to start searching for alternative solutions.

I'd say it's about time, nearly a century after they were first discarded, to rediscover these theories left on history's mantelpiece.

America On Coffee on July 26, 2015 at 11:18 am said:

AMERICA may endure the implementation of socialism, but it will be for a very brief time. And too, this 'crony' government will meet fierce resistance!
   Thank you for great political analysis.
   http://www.americaoncoffee10.WordPress.com

Paul mccrea on October 17, 2015 at 9:13 pm said:

Max, you have converted me from Marxism to Maxism! You show such a comprehensive analysis of the progression and regression of humanity and such wisdom. I am a friend of your aunt in Belfast and have shared your blog to my Facebook page. I am much older than you but your wisdom humbles me. Thank you for sharing it.

jackpkchadwick on October 26, 2015 at 10:58 pm said:

This is an interesting piece, I think it communicates the essence of Trotskyism very well. As someone who identifies with the ideas of Trotsky, what I've always also found intriguing was the latter's commitment to self-description as an 'Orthodox Marxist' and the materialist content of this term that – I personally think – marks the real boundary between Stalinism / ultra-Leftism, and Trotskyism. Trotsky explained the degeneration of the USSR in terms of the incompatibility of Russia's economic base – its material productive forces – with the socialist superstructure that Bolshevik's were prima facie committed to establishing. Under this view, the expulsion of Trotsky, the descent into Stalin's dictatorship, the betrayal of the October Revolution, were all historically necessary because of the aforementioned limitations. In more detail, the biggest concern of Trotsky was with the inefficiency of the method of centrally planning the economy. In the 1920s, to do this on the required scale needed an army of bureaucrats, with political power concentrated at the centre of this hive. Hence, the chief bureaucrats became a class of their own, the nomenklatura, presiding over an only partially socialist state. Contrasting this to the present, I think it's fair to say that the methods available for planning are increasingly plausible because of the developments in information technology; so were a period of crisis (such as that which precipitated the October Revolution) to occur, followed by a modern revolution led by a similar force to the Bolsheviks, I think the main risk of degeneration (Stalinist take-over) would be mitigated by the new set of tools available to a socialist government looking to establish democratic central planning.

23. COMMUNISM AND THE KURDISH QUESTION

Posted on July 31, 2015

Last Wednesday, a Turkish policeman made the headlines due to events on a street in the Diyarbakir region, eastern Turkey.

In a likely peaceful scene, it would seem improbable that Mehmet Uyar's conduct as a police officer would be required, and sitting in front of a teahouse, he probably didn't suspect anything. It was then, however, that a man shot at him from a car, wounding him and another innocent civilian (according to the news agencies Dogan and Anatolia).

Both were rushed to hospital, yet it was clear nothing could be done, and they soon died of their wounds. It is reported that another individual was also wounded in the shooting, though not fatally.

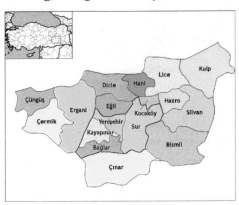

Here is the region in which the attack took place (Uyar was killed in the Cinar district)

This particular attack was blamed on the Kurdistan Worker's Party, a Kurdish militant movement of the radical Left, and (provided the allegations are correct) serves as another reminder of the Kurdish struggle in the region. As suggested by the movement's name, this struggle is oriented largely around the long-term goal of founding an independent country where Kurds may live free of oppression.* This is the topic I'll focus on today; the purpose of this entry is to look at the subject from a Marxist viewpoint.

To give my initial view, I do not support the struggle for an independent Kurdistan. To explain in detail why, and why I believe this to be the correct Marxist position to take, I'll examine the issue from two perspectives. The first will concern moral right and wrong (in the eyes of a Marxist), the second, Marxism itself...

Oppression against the Kurdish population is obviously a pressing issue, and I am wholly supportive of their liberation from tyranny, as well as their courageous fight against Islamic State. It is just the idea of a Kurdish nation that I'm inclined to oppose, for Kurdistan would be a state founded upon the presence of a prominent ethnicity; not only would this lead to discrimination (just look at Israel, a country founded as the homeland of the Jews, in which discrimination against the local Arabs is not only present, but often aggressive and violent) but would also distort the idea of genuine equality among racial groups, for the notion of Kurdistan proposes the 'shutting off' of the oppressed through the drawing of national boundaries. This would inevitably compromise any effort to achieve harmony between ethnic or racial groups, which, as an internationalist, I am strongly opposed to.

On the topic of Communism, I also have no doubt in saying that the former (or rather, the former's revolutionary implementation) would also be delayed by Kurdistan's existence, as whilst the emancipation of the Kurds is one thing, the emancipation of the proletariat is quite another. Thus, the ethnic struggle would only serve as a distraction from the real plight of the Kurdish underclasses.

A great example of a Marxist approach to these issues is Karl Marx's view on the tensions in nineteenth-century Ireland; although Marx did feel that the country would be better off without British rule, he believed that the national struggle in the soon-to-be republic would only prolong the Communist revolution in Britain.

I say this not just for the purposes of discussion, but also to other leftists who may sympathise with the national struggle. The Kurdistan Worker's Party, for example, would undoubtedly consider itself a Left-orientated organisation, yet is leading the fight for an independent racial country. I thus warn any socialists to beware of this trap – it may seem like a harmonious solution, but the founding of new states and the breaking-up of ethnic groups can only be a temporary one. In the long run, true equality will only be postponed.

*this idea was abandoned as a central idea of the party's leadership, yet was nonetheless one of its founding principles, and is still prominent in the region today

24. 'TIS THE SEASON TO REVOLT

Posted on August 7, 2015

What are the optimal conditions for revolution?

If asked this question, most Marxists would probably point to a strong, militant working class, an exploitative bourgeoisie to revolt *against*, and perhaps a period of warfare or hardship to initiate suffering of a kind sufficient to spark rebellion. There's reason behind this, for these were the conditions imagined by Karl Marx himself, which were present prior to many revolutions throughout the nineteenth and twentieth centuries, from the Paris Commune in France to the 26th July Movement in Cuba. However, whilst I wouldn't argue with any of these ideas, I believe that it's worth considering the question from other perspectives, for the circumstances of class and society are only the *social* conditions desired; they ignore whatever role the natural world may have in this process.

Though it may seem unlikely, evidence does suggest that our environment shapes our behaviour in a variety of odd ways, even creating circumstances where riots, rebellions and thus even revolutions are more likely to occur. It is known, for example, that rioting is more likely to occur in summer, when the air temperature is hotter and the population more agitated. An example would be the London riots of 2011, which took place primarily in the summertime as a reaction against police violence. Now, whilst short-lived and not in any way successful, it was a movement of considerable significance; not only was the wave of aggression a large-scale revolt which gained attention nationwide, but it was even thought to be revolutionary by certain people on the Left. Yet what happened when the season turned? The tensions cooled off with the weather, and the spirit of rebellion went out like a light.

Whilst these all effectively demonstrate how the weather can affect behaviour in this way, they are only one of multiple instances, for the coincidence of rebellion and hot weather is seen throughout history; the English Civil War broke out in the summer, as did the war in former-Yugoslav Slovenia, and the Tambov Rebellion in Soviet Russia. Perhaps the best exemplary country would be France, which has experienced much violence and revolutionary action in the past three centuries – a great deal in the summer months – from the Storming of the Bastille and the June Revolution to the events in Paris in 1968. And though the revolutionary or rebellious movements in England, France and Russia and Yugoslavia don't have a great deal in common, all follow a similar pattern, suggesting some correlation between hot weather and dissidence. Obviously, this tendency isn't consistent (the Russian October Revolution, for example, occurred at night during late autumn in a particularly cold part of the world) but it nonetheless supports the idea that a correlation exists.

Yet it isn't just the weather, various other occurrences in the natural world may actually contribute to the likelihood of revolution. For example evidence suggests that more crime is committed when there is a full moon. Two theories I've read claim this is because more people are out on the streets during the bright nights it provides, or possibly because the sky is lighter, making criminal behaviour more likely. It could also be a random correlation, with the moon having no actual role in stirring up criminal or rebellious behaviour, but it's worth considering. If it helps, the October Revolution occurred on the night of a bright moon, as did the spontaneous violence of Kristallnacht in Germany and the SA's rampage that sparked the Night of the Long Knives. The BBC News website also states that various police departments despatched more officers on full moon nights, in anticipation of increased criminal activity.

Revolution by moonlight... how romantic!

Many other factors will undoubtedly be involved, but take these as an introduction, a brief outline of the natural world's effect on revolutionary activity. It goes without saying that the social conditions, of class, suffering and oppression are far more important and far more likely to spark any kind of uprising, but it's worth bearing in mind that the right lighting and climate, alongside additional variables, may assist the rebellious cause. So, next time you're planning on initiating revolutionary war on capitalism, remember to plan the uprising during the summer months, and in case the struggle continues through the night, pick a time when the moon's full. After all, if the conditions around them had been different, many key failures in military history might have been successful.

25. THE 'C' WORD

Posted on August 28, 2015

There is much controversy surrounding the word I'm thinking of.

You don't hear it much out and about, but most know its meaning. It seems that it's always used in a negative way, often as an insult, and has been known to induce shock or offence (so much so that artistic expression of the concept is, in certain countries, considered so inappropriate that it's actually illegal). This is somewhat unusual, as it acquired the power to insult when it was never originally supposed to, and became synonymous with words and ideas to which it once bore no relation. In fact, when it first came into being, it was often associated with something rather wonderful, but if you tell someone today they're a complete c_____, I doubt you'll get a positive response.

Yes, Communism has been a controversial word for a long while. Somewhere down the line, it became a well-known enemy, and we saw it as such for the remainder of the twentieth century. We even created brilliant works of propaganda around the concept; perhaps it was coming to overthrow your democracy and install a dictatorial puppet state, or maybe it was (and there is truth behind this, though aggression was obviously far from one-sided) on the verge of flattening New York with a nine-megaton bomb, but it was a monster all the same. Society came to agree that whatever the Communists were planning, something bad would happen as a result.

The question is, however, when did this all start?

Ever since 1917, many saw in Communist Russia a foe. This can be traced back to the Allied intervention in the Russian Civil War, a conflict that occurred just after the catastrophic defeats of World War One. But the Communist terror and angst that would later plague Europe and North America was, at that point, largely nonexistent; in these early years, the west was largely unaware of both the political terror and the military challenge the regime would later provide, and thus, to call yourself a Communist probably didn't mean a great deal, for Communism was really just another radical idea. I once read an American newspaper headline at the time of the Russian Revolution, which described the Bolsheviks as 'extremists', comparing them with 'moderate governments' before them. Whilst I definitely felt anti-Bolshevik sentiment expressed there, the article implied nothing significant or special about their cause – the only distinction it drew between the party that would later lead their future nemesis and the easily forgotten Provisional Government, which assumed power for an eight-month period before October, was a mere statement that one was radical whilst the other was moderate.

In fact, many in the west were far more open to the prospect of Communism than this. George Bernard Shaw, for example, even advised the British unemployed to travel to the USSR, under the impression that they would be given a job. It's also known that the intelligentsia in the UK were a lot more sympathetic towards the Soviet Union than you might expect, and many respected their ideals in a way that would seem unimaginable during the years of the Cold War.

This continued throughout the repression of Stalin's era, and people still managed to find sympathy with his political system. I even heard that information regarding oppression in the Soviet Union was actually covered up by those able to do so, for fear that it might soil the image of Russia that many westerners undoubtedly clung to.

Only thirty or fourty years later, however, far from withdrawing information to preserve Soviet support, western governments would dress up and dramatise reality in the Eastern Bloc to an almost unfair level, printing McCarthyist slogans in black, probably against a red background and a hammer-and-sickle to add a sinister quality. After the 1917 revolution, tensions did occur between the Communist and capitalist worlds, but during the war something snapped, and relationships deteriorated almost to the level of sparking a World War Three. Communism, as a term, almost became synonymous with fascism, and I'm willing to bet that plenty don't know the difference, which is strange, given that only a few decades ago, this word would have accurately described the views of many in the west.

There isn't one explanation for the change, nor for why it occurred at that moment, and on reflection, it may seem odd that the Cold War began in 1945 and not 1917. After all, an obvious explanation for the post-war tensions is the lack of any need to preserve a situation of comradeship with the Soviet Union, once fascism had been finally

IS THIS TOMORROW

AMERICA UNDER COMMUNISM!

defeated, but nor was there a need to maintain diplomacy throughout the '20s and '30s. It would also be easy to assume that Communist aggression towards the west began only after the war, but this is again untrue; Lenin once referred to England as the Soviet Union's greatest enemy, and Soviet military action in the then British colony of India proves that such statements weren't at all hollow. So, as I understand it, there is only one reason why perceptions of Communism changed worldwide, and that is military prowess.

The USSR emerged from the war a highly capable country, and, if another conflict was to occur, the prospect of a western defeat was incredibly likely. Thus, though tyranny, repression and starvation were known prior to the war, they were largely ignored. Now that the west had a reason to fear the regime, a hatred for Communism was cultivated in no time with the assistance of these facts. Whilst writing, I'm aware that I've come across as critical towards Soviet Communism, and I am (by 'Soviet Communism', I mean the Soviet Union after 1924), yet I'm a Communist nonetheless, and I'm also critical of the west during this period, for I feel that the demonisation of Communism didn't occur due to the oppression and hardship it brought about where it was attempted, but to the fact that it provided a potential enemy. This highlights a disgusting aspect of the political situation in the western world – the opportunistic tendencies of democratic western governments, to ally or break with the worst kinds of states or governments when it suits their own interests, no matter how authoritarian, repressive, or simply *wrong* they may be (I'm not talking about a credible means-to-an-end kind of scenario – although this is likely a popular justification – I'm just talking about when it suits the interests of the international capitalists). To the western world, such an ideology wasn't evil from the start; it only became so when it threatened capitalism. This was why the 'C' word gathered such negativity. Not because of careful observation of socialism's many failures, but due to the material conditions the capitalist world found itself in. In short, it was it only when it actually stood a chance that Communism stopped being cool.

26. WORKERS, NOT MACHINES

Posted on September 4, 2015

We live in a world where our increasing reliance on technology is becoming ever more concerning.

Did you know that the University of Cambridge recently established a department on the protection of humanity from the threat of artificial intelligence? This isn't the only example; novels are written, films are produced, and serious debates and conversations worldwide discuss the subject, asking the same question that has worried mankind for decades: whether or not it's possible that some day, we will find ourselves at the mercy of machines.

Often, this is considered from a political perspective ('what if robots took over the world and reduced human beings to mere slaves?'), yet there's another side to the debate, for whilst having the potential for world domination, modern machinery could also revolutionise society's economy. Today, I'm asking whether or not the machines we build, quite capable of completing even the most menial tasks as efficiently as any human, take over the role of the industrial workforce.

It's definitely a question worth asking, because it could potentially threaten the careers of billions worldwide. It's also perfectly possible, unlike the subject of other debates surrounding robotics which concern an indefinite point in the future, when we have finally created artificial intelligence or some other development we can't actually be sure we'll achieve. No, this is something that could happen in a matter of years – we have the technology, probably the money, to allow it to occur – all we need is the will. So, given how likely this would be, it would be sensible to assume that the capitalist world can look forward to a new age of human development; that some day soon, we'll have a worker-free economy.

Or is it?

As a Marxist, this question has troubled me, because it suggests that humans are very close to achieving capitalism without exploitation. In the Communist Manifesto, Marx and Engels wrote of a similar idea, which they referred to as 'Conservative, or Bourgeois Socialism', explaining how 'The Socialistic Bourgeois want all the advantages of modern social conditions without the struggles and dangers necessarily resulting therefrom. They desire the existing state of society minus its revolutionary and disintegrating elements. They wish for a bourgeoisie without a proletariat.'

Now, the Communist Manifesto, arguably the document around which Communism is centred, dismisses such a utopian proposition, as did I when reading it; it contradicts the key Marxian idea that exploitation of the international proletariat may only end after a proletarian revolution, suggesting that capitalism can be made 'friendly'. Thus, when I realised that it would seem logical for new developments in technology to allow just that, I considered how I'd approach this idea, not wanting the entire basis for my philosophy to be disproven. I eventually decided why (in my opinion, at least) it won't happen...

1. This Could Have Happened Years Ago

One thing I realised was that the replacement of an industrial proletariat with machinery or robots isn't an idea entirely unique to today's world, for machinery has played a key role in industry since Marx's day. In fact, one of his most important theories (the theory of Relative Surplus Value) argues that the rate of profit accumulation can only change through reorganisation of the workforce, which may include the introduction of machines or new technologies. In short, I believe that if mechanisation was a goal the capitalists really wanted to go for, they'd surely have done it by now.

It could be argued that, until modern times, this wasn't possible, as only recently have we developed technology capable of performing the advanced tasks necessary to society today. But whilst machines have caught up with us in this respect, many of the basic tasks that theoretically could have been left to machinery back in Marx's day, weren't. Even back then, it would have been possible to build machines that would have eliminated many of the most basic and menial tasks carried out by the proletariat, but this, largely didn't happen. Similarly, it's possible to eradicate a great deal more of the tasks fulfilled by today's workers, but if we follow in the same trend, I don't see why this will occur today either.

It all comes down to the same principle, which is that, given the current circumstances, it's just easier to employ workers than invest in technology. To quote Mike Daisey's 'The Agony and the Ecstasy of Steve Jobs', a monologue about the conditions of those who produce Apple products in Shenzhen, China, 'why use machines when you can use people?' Now, there are accusations that some of what Daisey describes has been fabricated for effect, but this doesn't matter in this instance, as the argument is the same: it's often easier to exploit the life out of ten, fifteen or five million than it is to rely on expensive and perhaps-not-always-available technologies that may perform the same task.

The workers of Shenzhen

2. If It Did Happen, It Would Only Be Temporary
Let's imagine for a second that it happened; that the economy was transformed by robotics. I'd like to point out that there is a serious problem with non-human elements taking over

140

the workforce, for we forget that we live in a society of man. This may seem obvious, but it's important to remember, for, in the world we've created, humans require jobs. If, after the 'technological revolution', machinery replaces the roles of the modern-day proletariat, everyone except the wealthy middle and upper classes is thrown out of work... and they're going to need employment.

It's hard to imagine exactly what this would lead to, but if you imagine billions of people who can't work, and thus don't have a source of income, it's not hard to see that some kind of crisis will result. The way I see it, it would likely mean one of two things: either we'd be forced to take a sharp U-turn away from mechanisation in an attempt to reintroduce capitalism as we know it, allowing society to progress more or less in the way Marx predicted, or we'd see something like the biggest and most dramatic revolution in history and capitalism would be destroyed altogether (again giving Marxism significant credibility). Either that or three billion would starve to death.

You may be thinking 'surely, no one would let it get *that* bad!' and I agree, which brings me to my third and final argument: I don't believe that we, society, would let this come to be...

3. It Wouldn't Happen in the First Place

I can't imagine mankind being so blind to the possibility of all the above occurring. Forget Marxism, forget revolution, and just imagine that three billion or so, a figure which no benefits service, no welfare system, no charity in the world could cater for. Will we just watch these people get thrown out of work, one by one?

When discussing this issue with somebody, they offered a counter-argument suggesting that such change would be gradual, and would take place only in the form of different brands, companies and factories starting to introduce new technologies to compete with one another. This is likely true, but the results, like the process, would also appear gradually. Therefore, as rising unemployment can't be seen as a good result by any measure, this would only give us time to pause and think. To end our short-lived dream of a bourgeoisie without a proletariat. To stop what we're doing before that figure gains nine zeros.

Russ on October 18, 2015 at 7:01 pm said:

Great blog, and article.
I wonder if some of the cracks are already appearing in the current system. Contra corner, a blog by David Stockman, gives insight into how the US has failed to create any net new jobs since 2000.

Maintaining the current system and balance of power has relied upon a massive expansion of credit since we moved off the gold standard in the 70s, and this has allowed the US to pursue foreign policy objectives through economic means.

The latest credit bubble is the biggest yet, and has resulted in the biggest misallocation of funds the world has seen. Ironically efficient allocation of resources is historically the thing that capitalism has been good at, but which socialism has struggled with.

27. TERRORISM AND COMMUNISM

Posted on September 11, 2015

Terrorism and Communism: a book by Leon Trotsky, 1920

Since the 9/11 attacks, fourteen years ago to this day, terrorism has become a major international concern.

This isn't to say that it didn't play a role prior to the fall of the Twin Towers; in the UK, many feared the Irish Republican Army (IRA); in Peru, it was the Shining Path; and of course, various Islamic attacks like the Lockerbie bombing were carried out before 2001. But after the end of the Cold War, when the capitalist world's greatest threat had been defeated, you could say that those who waged war with home-built bombs and illegally bought Kalashnikovs were once again brought into focus. Now that this form of warfare has once again established itself as a serious threat, perhaps one of the greatest threats to society's wellbeing, I'm looking at where Communism fits in with it all.

In fact, many of today's terrorist organisations fight for a socialist future. These include the Unified Communist Party of Nepal, the Maoist terrorist organisations in India, and, as mentioned above, the leftist militants in Peru. The actions attributed to them range from destroying buildings to kidnapping influential people (this was done famously by the Red Brigades' kidnapping and murder of former Italian prime minister Aldo Moro), all with Marxism in mind. But though these people may act in Communism's name, they don't have a great history of success in that regard. Can you

143

name a time when a country has been overthrown altogether by an act of terrorism, let alone Communist terrorism?

By its very nature, terrorist practice involves individuals or organisations committing acts of aggression to advance their goals, and these actions have, throughout history, always been shocking but often not particularly productive. The destruction of buildings in India, the kidnapping of a politician in Italy, or the burning of ballot boxes in Peru (all of which have been done in the past) may be cruel, murderous or evil, but it's not as though they solve a great deal. Often, it seems to me that these actions are no more than pointless violence.

The logo of the organisation that killed Moro

However, there are obvious exceptions to this: if we consider terrorism in a general sense, it could be argued that the ANC would not have gained the attention of the South African public had it not been for its criminal actions, or that votes for women would not have been granted had the Suffragettes not vandalised streets. It's thus possible that socialism's revolutionary aims may be realised through terrorism of some sort, and therefore, whilst it's so often unsuccessful and relatively useless, I can't dismiss the concept entirely; the success stories above prevent me from doing so.

This is why I'm left in the middle of the road, a political position I almost never find myself in. I don't condone terrorism regardless, as it's often likely to do no more than cultivate hatred for you and your motive whilst damaging property or lives in the process, but nor do I condemn it – it can be used to produce brilliant outcomes (as we've seen in the examples of black liberation and women's rights). As to whether such actions will work for this motive in particular, *Communist* terrorists are unlucky in the sense that they fight for an unpopular goal. Its unpopularity is unfair, I believe, but does exist all the same, and thus, these actions may only confirm prior suspicions that Communism is good for nothing but inducing suffering.

All I can say is that leftists out there must be careful. This manner of war can work, and can be justified, but only if it really does establish change. It may be difficult to tell when this is the case; the misdeeds of the IRA merely shocked the public and shamed the Republican struggle, whereas those of the Suffragettes proved crucial to their cause. Without careful consideration of the circumstances, it's likely that a few groups and organisations will do nothing but harm our common cause.

28. COMMUNISM, NOT CORBYNISM

Posted on September 18, 2015

Last week, something significant happened in the world of politics: Britain's once moderate and reformist Labour Party elected an anti-monarchist, Trade Union-backed socialist as their leader, who aims to bring key industries back into state control, leave NATO and create a socialist United Kingdom (/Republic). Given that this was the party which, only eighteen years ago was advocating a kind of social capitalism, it's possible that they've never had a leader this radical.

Can you imagine the kind of fuss this will cause if he wins the general election? The western Left has become so moderate in recent years, with even capitalistic centrists like Barack Obama having been accused of 'socialism', that it's as though there's no longer a place for the Corbynites of this world. The USA (a country not only less-to-the-left, but more-to-the-right as well), is an even better example. If J.C. rose to president in America, there'd probably be a second civil war!

However, in the midst of all this, it's important that the Marxist Left remember something: Corbyn is not as radical as you may be inclined to believe. OK, maybe in a country like the UK, where former party leader Ed Milliband qualifies as a 'f***ing Communist' (courtesy Noel Gallagher), his views could be seen as extreme, but this is only in comparison to what we're used to; not socialism, but watered-down capitalism.

Corbyn lies between the two, and this, I think, presents a problem. He's no Milliband, but nor is he Marx. In the words of his deputy, Tom Watson, 'Jeremy Corbyn is not a Trotskyist' and 'Liz Kendall is not a Tory', and in the same sense that the reluctance of his former opposition is certainly noted and perhaps exaggerated, so are his ideas, perhaps to the point where the radical Left could mistake him for 'one of them'. In reality, I'd say he's more of an in-the-middle leftist, a political island between social democracy and Communism; a radical moderate. And as a result, I believe he'll do more harm than good. Here's why:

There is a certain side to the British Left that is largely destructive. The trade-unionist movement is an example, for, unlike those of genuinely radical socialists, their ideas aren't scientific, they don't stand on concrete principles, they aren't guided by a clear motive of socialism, and they are, in a way, directionless. Devoid of a clear plan, these movements criticise, attack, threaten and whine about the way things are, and they do so marvellously, but what do they contribute? As far as I'm concerned, not a great deal. OK, minor alterations have been made to the economy as a result of their existence, yet, as these movements are still intertwined with the capitalist system, I'd still see their role as counter-productive.

Corbyn falls in this camp, as do those who elected him, for they attack capitalism yet won't commit to a Communist alternative. It's a bit like igniting a revolution but refusing to build a solution to the society you destroyed, which begs the question 'why revolt?' True, Labour will likely plan to transform the economy in certain ways, such as the renationalisation of industry, yet firstly, simply because an institution exists under state control doesn't necessarily make it any less exploitative, and secondly, any attempts they do make could easily be undone by whoever replaces them.

If that day comes around (if he's voted in in the first place, which he won't be), Corbyn, the 'extremist', the 'Trotskyite', the 'revolutionary' etc., will leave office in a country just as capitalistic as it was before, yet with an economy in shambles and a reinforced hatred for socialism.

It doesn't need saying that, irrespective of whatever views you may have, neither will do us any good.

Stephen Twist on October 9, 2015 at 3:36 pm said:

'Such categories as "commodity", "money", "wages", "capital", "profit", "tax'" and the like are only semi-mystical reflections in men's heads of the various aspects of a process of economy which they do not understand and which is not under their control. To decipher them, a thoroughgoing scientific analysis is indispensable'. – Trotsky

Reuben on October 10, 2015 at 7:52 pm said:

I'd like to start by saying that I really love your blog, and since I was introduced to it a couple of weeks ago I have been working back through your posts. They are filled with a huge amount of insight and are impeccably argued.

   I would like though, to argue against a number of points you make in this post.

   Firstly, you attack the trade union movement as an example of a part of the British Left which is 'purely destructive'. How can you ignore the vast contribution that trade unions have made to our society in the past century? Everything from abolishing child labour over a century ago to forcing the Labour Party into the minimum wage in '97 are down to the unions as well as contributing to the enactment of the welfare state and NHS, equal pay for both genders etc. Now the obvious response to this is to say that in the past unions were helpful but now the unions are merely a nuisance which has not won anything since Thatcher. Certainly the trade union movement (as with all of the British Left) is going through a tough time with less members than the past, but this does not mean that unions cannot fight for workers rights. Over the past five years unions have won and lost but there have been significant gains for some workers like the Ritzy cinema staff, tube drivers, UCL cleaners (sorry those are all in London, it's because that's where I'm based), the list goes on. What makes you think that unions have a detrimental effect on society? They may not be in a good place at the moment, but it is far better that they exist than if they didn't.

   Obviously, unions are mediators between workers and capitalism, so in the event of a revolutionary struggle they would have to give way to a revolutionary party or other organisation to organise the workers, but under capitalism they provide a huge benefit to working people which we cannot simply ignore because occasionally they annoy us by not fighting their cause enough.

I would also like to challenge your assertion that Corbyn is destructive to the Left. Let us be clear about what Corbyn is and what he represents. He is not, as you say, against capitalism, he is against neoliberalism, and the solution he is presenting (not socialism, you are correct) is social democracy. Although he may be further to the Left than the policies he is presenting, the policy platform he is putting forward or has put forward so far is about making capitalism kinder to the poorest.

Yes, this is not revolutionary, and I don't think that he is going to cause a revolt and then be left with a smouldering country and no alternative. The British Left has got to take these things one step at a time, shifting debate slowly to the Left until we find ourselves in a revolutionary situation. This is a slow process, and we are certainly not ready for revolution just yet in the midst of the hegemonic neoliberal project. We need to begin by getting away from this extreme strain of capitalism, and the first step of this is to move to a more reformed version of capitalism. That is what Jeremy Corbyn is providing us with. It is an opportunity to move one step leftwards to change the debate around the neoliberal shrinking of the state and austerity.

He may not be the next Lenin, but we've got to support him.

The Anonymous Revolutionary on October 12, 2015 at 3:08 pm said:

I really like your argument, and understand the point you made about the unions (I agree that they're not purely destructive and have edited that part of the post), but still think that they lack clear direction and ideological aim, and thus don't serve a productive purpose in the way of ending exploitation (I think I explained that better in the section I edited).

I think this is perhaps the main reason why we disagree on Corbyn, because I'm looking at this from a Marxist perspective and am talking of building Communism in a permanent and revolutionary sense. This is why I'm very cautious to embrace Corbyn's ideas, because I believe capitalism cannot be eroded away through a gradual process, and that, by reforming our economic system we may well only be prolonging it. If it was a choice between reformed capitalism or neoliberalism, I'd choose the former, but I uphold that a third, Communist alternative is achievable, and that compromise will not help us in that regard.

Reuben on November 5, 2015 at 9:30 am said:

Sorry it has taken me a while to reply to this, I really appreciate you taking the time to reply.

Surely you believe though that we are not currently in a revolutionary situation. If you agree that the revolution is not going to happen (in the UK at least) in the short term, then we have to consider how we (as the Left) move to this revolutionary situation. One of the best ways, in my opinion, to do this is through repeated wins within capitalism – if we keep on demanding better and better conditions and less exploitation within capitalism, then at some point we encounter a limit. It is at that point, when we can no longer better our lives within capitalism that we then overthrow capitalism.

In addition, it is only through education and politicisation and the politics of socialism becoming more talked about that we can achieve a class consciousness which is necessary for revolution.

Surely then, Jeremy Corbyn is the first step in both of these ongoing goals for the Left, which will eventually result in a revolutionary situation.

29. A MEANS TO AN END (OF EXPLOITATION): MARXISM AND UTILITARIANISM

Posted on September 26, 2015

Over the past hundred years, I won't deny that many ruthless and otherwise unjustifiable acts have been carried out in the name of socialism. Sometimes, these actions were directly harmful (such as the use of state terror), whereas in other examples they were not (such as the introduction of strict economic policies that later caused suffering), yet many perished all the same. This is why Communists today require adequate justification for what's been going on in these countries, and it would seem to me that this comes most naturally in the argument that the end may justify the means, or if you're Trotsky, 'the end may justify the means so long as there is something that justifies the end' (I know it sounds slightly pretentious).

This is a core idea of utilitarianism, an ethical theory predating Marxism, which argues in a very general sense that an action is defined in terms of its consequences. Thus even concepts like genocide, which we'd normally consider horrific, are permissible if they bring about greater happiness than would have otherwise been the case, the principle of the greatest happiness for the greatest number of people lying at the heart of the philosophy. Just from this, one can see key similarities between Marxist and utilitarian thought; they both exist with an eye to the majority; they both strive for the wellbeing of the masses, and in both schools of thought it is upheld that violence, be it in the case of class conflict (Marxism) or the 'Trolley Problem' (utilitarianism), may be used to achieve the greater good. So I'm writing to discuss the similarities between these two philosophies, whether or not Marxism can operate in a utilitarian way – or vice versa – and finally, whether or not utilitarianism successfully justifies the many otherwise-atrocious actions committed in Communism's name.

First of all, it's worth pointing out that Marx's ideas entail an element of sacrifice. Friedrich Engels once stated that 'The next world war will result in the disappearance from the face of the earth not only of reactionary classes and dynasties, but also of reactionary peoples', and the fact that he followed this up with 'this too, will be a step forward' confirms the utilitarian character of such thinking, which treated these horrors as a necessary part of the Communist struggle. On top of this, it has to be remembered that Marx's interpretation of what capitalism would inevitably lead to, whilst a *scientific* interpretation, also bore the label of justice, equality and all that was right. Thus, science and morality merged with the Marxian prediction that from capitalism there would arise Communism, the latter being a better moral alternative as well as an inevitable one. This was simply because it upheld the idea of a better world, the best, in fact, of all hitherto economic systems (except possibly Primitive Communism). True, that's an incredibly vague interpretation, but I think it's obvious that the specific ideas of classlessness or an end of exploitation are credited as they result in a happier society. This is why the Greatest Happiness

Principle, as it's called, is definitely present in scientific Marxism and underpins the core Marxist ideas and theories.

If we can thus accept that these ideas are utilitarian ones, I think it's also true that they are justified in a utilitarian way. The kind of violence Marx and Engels spoke of wasn't without reason; why would anybody advocate ruthlessness when they didn't feel it was necessary? And when I talk of its necessity, I refer to progression – forward movement in the direction of liberty and equality – towards greater happiness. It could be argued that Marxism is not a science and that Communism is not an absolute truth, so therefore there's nothing to justify what has been done in its name. Firstly, whether or not Marx was right is a separate debate, and secondly, even if Marx was proven wrong; even if we find that there is no inevitability in Communism, such a brilliant concept is surely still worth fighting for.

I conclude by saying that Marxism's utilitarian nature should be realised, as the two theories will likely benefit from what the other has to provide; currently, whilst many do acknowledge why Marx's ideas should be vindicated, many don't, and a sturdy, underlying justification would do a good job in providing a simple explanation in this regard. I think it's even possible to argue that, similarly, utilitarianism lends itself to a Marxist interpretation, due to the values it places on the state of the majority in society above all else – also an idea worth exploring. The political views of Jeremy Bentham, one of, if not the most important figure in the founding and development of contemporary utilitarianism, reflect this.

Richard Armstrong on October 12, 2015 at 11:39 am said:

I think your most recent blog (Oct 9) is extremely brave and I have a huge amount of respect for you. My thoughts are with you and your family at this time.

I thought your piece on Utilitarianism and Marxism was really well written and excellently argued. I am sure that you have more important things to consider at this time than my comments below, but if you need something to keep you occupied then I have set out below one of the problems that I have always had with Marxism.

If we put to one side philosophical objections to utilitarianism (virtue ethics, religion, existentialist ethics, liberalism etc.) then I suppose the fundamental question is whether Marxism could indeed lead to the greatest happiness for the greatest number. My instincts are that the level of state authority required to create and maintain a Marxist economic order would always reduce the sum total of happiness by more than the resulting economic justice would increase it, because people value individual liberty freedom above material conditions – but then it is easy for someone living in the prosperous West to take that view. I suppose the 'individual liberty' that I enjoy is the freedom to enjoy a high standard of living at the expense of others. Is this a point you have considered?

I completely understand if you don't reply to this post. Well done again on the excellent blog. Inspirational stuff.

Richard

The Anonymous Revolutionary on October 12, 2015 at 4:58 pm said:

Thank you so much and I really like your point – it's something I really considered when I was thinking about whether Marxism and utilitarianism are compatible.

Ultimately, I'd say that whilst capitalism strives to create happiness for a minority (at the expense of an exploited majority), socialism does so for a majority (at the expense of an exploitative minority) so utilitarian ideas still apply. True, the creation of a centralised economy will lead to a loss of some happiness as it restricts individual liberties when they clash with popular interests, but I believe that happiness of this sort is only possible at the expense of these interests, so a socialist redistribution of wealth does exemplify the Greatest Happiness Principle. It's also worth remembering that Communism entails the idea of a classless society, and thus encourages economic liberties in the sense that it seeks to end all career-based regimentation and promotes individual leisure.

Obviously, this is a theoretical ideal, and you could argue that, in practice, Communism leads to a net loss of happiness in society. I'd argue that even if we can be certain this has been the case in Communist countries, we shouldn't let socialism be defined by these early attempts at equality, and that we should recognise the true values and ideas Communism stands upon.

30. MARXISM, OPIUM AND MORPHINE

Posted on October 9, 2015

It's been an intense week.

Last Wednesday I was told of a tumour in my spine after experiencing some pain and immobility in my neck and right arm. I was operated on the following day (coincidentally the sixty-sixth anniversary of the 1949 Chinese Revolution) and have since been bed-bound and unable to do a great deal, this being the reason why I didn't post last Friday. The bonus is the fact that the food in Leeds General Infirmary is actually quite good, and the downside is, well… cancer, but it can't be helped; it's the problem with having naturally revolutionary cells.

Between last Wednesday and now I've worried about various things, but one thought that stands out is religion. Before I go into more depth, I'll stress that I'm an atheist. Religion, the way I see it, is a reactionary and backward tendency that has stood alongside man throughout history, yet has always blinded communities and corrupted rational thought. As society has advanced, so has our depth of knowledge and understanding of the world and, as a result, religious influence has decreased in many ways, but that's not to say it isn't an issue. The Israeli-Palestinian conflict, the persisting cultural backwardness in the southern USA, and the political situation in Iraq, Saudi Arabia and Iran are all different manifestations of the same illness. Religion does to society what cancer is doing to my spine.

And then, of course, there is another side to this kind of faith, this being comfort, the reason it exists in the first place. I think it's obvious that if it wasn't for how deeply these spiritual teachings have already impacted upon our histories and cultures, we (in a much wiser era) would be far less easily convinced by the arguments they have to offer today, and the most important reason why mankind still clings to these outdated ideas is the sense of safety and security they continue to provide. Religion is an effective distraction and an inviting alternative to the harsh realities of day-to-day life, and this is why we swallow it today just like we've done for centuries. It is, in the language of Marx, opium for the masses, just like the oral morphine I've been taking to deal with post-operative pain (although unlike Islam, Christianity or Judaism, I'm still baffled as to why people develop addictions to this substance – I can't say I've noticed it make more difference than paracetamol!)

Yet this is where God comes into my story, because, just as I've swallowed the morphine, I've also been praying: my prayers tending to follow the lines of 'Dear God, if you exist, I'd be so grateful if you would show mercy'. This isn't to say I'm any more convinced of God's existence than I was last month; I just took the view that it was worth it, in case I'm wrong. I know religious people who have prayed for me, too, and I welcome their thoughts and prayers as well, despite feeling slightly hypocritical, given my own vehement atheism. If God does exist, I'd rather be spared than damned, and I see no wrong in telling him, even though rationality tells me there's nobody on the other side of the void. And, after all, while mainstream Marxism rejects religious influence in societal matters, it doesn't necessarily reject private beliefs. In the end, I suppose I'm only harming my pride.

As it happens, I have little reason to believe there's a lot going on in heaven for me. On Wednesday I was told that my cancer, on a I – IV grading system, fell into the most aggressive, Grade IV category. No one could commit to giving me a death date, but I'm left with the impression that, after chemotherapy, radiotherapy and physiotherapy (to regain movement), all of which should begin next week, I'll have months to live. This was obviously terrible news, though it perhaps takes some of the pressure off as it makes me more assured in my godlessness, and I also can't help but feel slightly proud that it's my spinal cells which have done this. In revolutionary terms, they definitely qualify as extremists. They'd dwarf the various coups in Argentina, which overthrew and replaced different governments there, or the revolutionary movements in the Communist countries like Vietnam or Afghanistan. My cells certainly take after the Bolsheviks here; if the February Revolution was my initial diagnosis, the October Revolution was my conversation two days ago. The shooting of the Romanov family is yet to come, but we're sure these cells will take no prisoners there either. It's also interesting to see that, due to their rapid growth and malignancy, they follow in the internationalist line, bent on spreading the revolution worldwide. Ideologically speaking, I can't really complain.

But meanwhile, I'll probably keep trying these things. It seems the logical option to utilise the means you have, in the hope that something may change. I certainly don't feel any sensible reason why anything will, but our complete lack of evidence on the subject makes it just as possible as ridiculous, so it would be irrational to rule out ideas of God, heaven or the metaphysical world entirely. And, whilst still a card-carrying member of the physical one, I'll hopefully keep reading, studying and blogging.

I suppose we'll just have to see how it goes from there...

Brian Dunning on October 12, 2015 at 8:31 pm said:

Dear Max, putting aside any beliefs ideological or otherwise, the most important thing for you is to believe that you can survive. I was diagnosed with an incurable form of leukaemia 15 years ago and I am still here. The doctors are as impressed as I am. One fact I remember from the outset was that I was told that anyone who came out fighting from the start could expect to live 50% longer than someone who threw in the towel. I have been in remission for three years now since my last bout of chemo and feel very good. Come out fighting Max, don't give in, best wishes, Brian

The Anonymous Revolutionary on October 12, 2015 at 8:38 pm said:

Thanks so much, and I definitely agree that I've got to keep fighting. You might have read Stephen J. Gould's 'The Median is not the Message'. This was an essay about cancer and survival I came across that also really helped. Best wishes, Max

edwardbindloss on October 13, 2015 at 10:49 am said:

Max,
I read your blog with interest and the news of your

cancer with great sadness. Your father sent me this link (I was at university with him and law school with both your parents and you came to my wedding when you were 3 days old).

What I really liked in your post was the stoicism with which you write about your situation and the ironic humour shown about the revolutionary cancer cells maintaining ideological consistency with your Marxism. I also wanted to develop your point about religion. You write, as an materialist atheist, that religion has corrupted rational thought but nevertheless you have been praying just in case. The French philosopher Pascal called this strategy his wager, and he regarded it as entirely rational. Pascal's wager is this: it is wise for an person to wager that God exists, since 'If you gain, you gain all; if you lose, you lose nothing.' Like you I am an atheist, but the fact that you are praying is, according to Pascal, the wise thing to do. So I don't think it should harm your pride at all.

I see from some of the other comments here that you are referred to as brave. My mother died young from cancer and people kept calling her brave, but she said to them 'I have no choice in this situation and so that is not real bravery.' In your case your stoicism, humour, fighting spirit and (Pascalian) wisdom is, to me, what is impressive and admirable. I wanted to write and say this and tell you that you are in my thoughts (as are your parents).

I look forward to your further posts and I wish you well.

Edward

Scott Sullivan on October 13, 2015 at 2:07 pm said:

Well Max – Your writing belies your young age. Your fortitude and courage are simply inspirational. Keep writing Max, I am very much looking forward to more posts. Most of your analogies make perfect sense to me. My hope is that the parallel you draw with your reactionary cells will continue until some capitalist forces rise up and contain your Bolshevik cells. What we need now is a White Army to stem the tide… And buy some time for a Reagan and (dare I say) the Iron Lady herself. Funny what you root for, or turn to in a crisis. – Scott Sullivan

PS. Couldn't agree more with your thoughts about the US South. We northerners call them 'Crackers'.

PPS. Communism doesn't work, because people like to own stuff – Frank Zappa

Malcolm Tolladay on October 13, 2015 at 11:17 pm said:

Max, You are not only an inspirational writer, but an inspiration to us all. I felt compelled to seek a way to respond to your blog by turning to perhaps one of the most famous revolutionaries who still happens to live in our times…

Fidel Castro said 'Revolution is not a bed of roses. Revolution is a battle between the future and the past'

Incredibly, it has been reported that over the years Castro has survived over 638 assassination attempts, yet in August this year he has just celebrated his 89th birthday! This certainly gives a great illustration of how someone can defy all the odds. We are all with you and behind you in the revolution for your future! – Malcolm Tolladay

Caitlin Hankey on October 14, 2015 at 1:18 pm said:

Max – difficult to find the right words after reading this piece! Magnificent in all respects – certainly a challenge to read and digest – but definitely focused my mind on two particular elements you mention – the power and role of HOPE, and the wayward paths LIFE FORCES can lead us down. For you, I shall now focus my energies on a counter-revolution of equal character! Look forward to the next blog :) Caitlin

anne monk on October 14, 2015 at 8:41 pm said:

Hi Max, I'm the other Marxist in your epq if you can remember me :) I'm so so sorry to hear about your cancer, my thoughts are with you and I am hoping for your recovery! Your writing is exceptional and you are without a doubt the most politically thoughtful person I have come across of our age, I am inspired by your writing and think that you have a great gift. Your motivation and determination is amazing, keep it up! :)

The Anonymous Revolutionary on October 15, 2015 at 7:20 pm said:

Hi Anne, thank you so much and it's great to hear from you! Keep up the struggle against capitalism (:

Mark W on October 15, 2015 at 8:24 am said:

Dear Max, I don't know you (I know your uncle Adrian), but my thoughts are with you. I hope that if I got a diagnosis like yours I would respond with the same courage, realism and humour, but I somehow doubt I would manage it.

I used to take the same view as you of religion, and it certainly has a lot to answer for, but I've grown more tolerant of it. Perhaps it is possible to understand religious stories, even if not as literally true, as metaphors, signposts that point to something – something about our common humanity, about holiness for want of a better word, that we don't have a more direct language to express. For an atheist I've sat in a lot of church services – it comes with singing in choirs – and I've seen that for some people religion is a way of understanding our place in the world that inspires and helps them to appreciate good things, value and consider others, experience a sense of wonder, but also to deal with with bad or even terrible things. And besides, as you say, we never know for sure: perhaps we're wrong and it's all true. I'm a lefty like you, not that I think 1917 was a great advert for Marxism all told, but anyway, if your immune system is the Tsarist secret police and the doctors are the Allied powers, I'll be praying that this time the Romanovs make it.

Robert Watson on October 15, 2015 at 9:49 am said:

Oh Lord…If there is a Lord.

Save my soul…If I have a soul.
Keep up the good fight.

Georgina Humphrey on October 15, 2015 at 1:08 pm said:

Max,
I am ashamed to say that my google history would throw up things like:
   Who does the voiceovers on Peppa Pig?
   How many calories in a Double Decker?
   And more recently, Are Ugg boots really out of fashion?
   So much time is spent on mindless trivia.
   It doesn't make us feel informed or enlightened!
   And yet this week, I felt both those things and I have you to thank!
   This week I googled The Collected Works of Lenin, The life and works of Leon Trotsky
   And….Faux Fur Gillets (sorry….you can take the girl out of Liverpool…I'm working on that).
   I am quite fascinated by the principles and ideas behind communism in its truest sense….sure I had to look up half your references but finally a google history to be proud of!
   Max, you are a great thinker, a brilliant writer and above all you have the quality of all great revolutionaries…the ability to inspire!
   In the words of my new Google Buddy Leon Trotsky:
   'The depth and strength of a human character are defined by its moral reserves.

People reveal themselves completely only when they are thrown out of the customary conditions of their life, for only then do they fall back on their reserves.'

Max, you couldn't be further from the customary conditions of your life and the depth and strength of your character could not be shining more brightly.

Thank you for inspiring us all

We are all waiting with eager anticipation for your next blog....

Jenny Holton on October 15, 2015 at 5:16 pm said:

Hi Max,

I really enjoyed reading your blog. It was very thought provoking. It is a very, very long time since I read your work and it is very, very different from Year 3! We are all thinking of you at Scarcroft. You are so brave and we have put you on our 'inspirational' wall in the staffroom. Keep writing.

Jenny Holton

Loreto ValenzuelaL on October 15, 2015 at 5:20 pm said:

(third attempt) My texts seems to disappear:

Dear Max,

This is my second attempt, I wrote once this morning but the text disappeared.

I send you some pictures on a text Loreto Adrian's friend.

Wow! you have such a revolutionary blood

running through your vain!!! and an inspiring writer.

Your writings reminded me of my youth, back in Santiago, Chile in the 80's when we were under the horrible regime, dictatorship. Although I was no near your braveness, inspiring, elocutionary and articulated as you are now. I found myself reading Lenin's Manifesto which some would say the cousin of Marx but it is more really like his son. More than with his writings (Lenin's) I was more concerned with the colours of those day which were certainly mainly on the grey scale and somehow the manifesto helped to some of us to have a breath of an alternative and hope.

Like your writings, which a refreshing breeze of bravery and persistence. There you also reminded me of a book (which I'm afraid I have not read) but I watched the movie, The Martians (a novel) by Andy Weil. Your persistence is like the persistence and passion of the protagonist Mark Watney. He kept going, this was the only way, I guess that is the best you can do! and gosh you do well. If you have not read it let me know and I send it to you.

Your God thoughts touched me totally too, as there are many times that I have toyed with what I think is one of these paradoxes, self referential in this case: If it does, then it does not! and if it does not, then does! you get the idea I hope.

With revolutionary hopes and how they say: Keep writing Comrade!

love, Loreto

Ruthie on October 16, 2015 at 12:11 pm said:

Hi Max,

I'm sorry to hear this is happening to you just at the (possible) dawning of the new socialist utopia. Socialism now exists as a political force in the UK and Europe once again having been all but invisible for 30 years. A whole generation has grown up with the belief that neo-liberalism is the only viable system. It is heartwarming to see so many younger people now waking up to the possibility of a socialist alternative, and the the realisation that voting can change things. Whilst there is a still a long road to travel, it is an exciting novelty to be part of a broader political debate.

On the God question, I have cycled through belief and atheism to settle, at least for the moment, as an agnostic. Since God, if he/she/it exists is all-knowing, all-seeing and everlasting, it knows our struggles on the matter of belief and our thoughts even before we think them.

Since humans tend to anthropomorphise everything there is a tendancy to think of God in human terms. Since we now know that time is not an absolute and the universe exists in multiple dimensions I think it is entirely possible that God exists but simply in a form that we are incapable of comprehending. I hope that death will be a passage of sublimation into some higher consciousness at which point all these issues with which we grapple will become clear.

I recently spent a weekend in a convent with a group of cloistered nuns, one of whom made a

comment which touched me deeply,
   'We really have very little control over what happens to us.' Which for someone like me who tends to feel responsible for everything, came as a glorious relief.

Mike Williamson on October 18, 2015 at 11:10 pm said:

Hi Max,
I don't know you or your family at all, but a friend drew my attention to your blog. I too am a socialist atheist. I started questioning religion in a serious way when one of my friends died in a motorcycle accident in my teens. He was completely innocent and it seemed so unfair. I imagine your loved ones will feel the same way about your predicament. This was before Dawkins had turned full islamophobe so I took great comfort in his words, from the opening of Unweaving the Rainbow:
   'We are going to die, and that makes us the lucky ones. Most people are never going to die because they are never going to be born. The potential people who could have been here in my place but who will in fact never see the light of day outnumber the sand grains of Arabia. Certainly those unborn ghosts include greater poets than Keats, scientists greater than Newton. We know this because the set of possible people allowed by our DNA so massively exceeds the set of actual people. In the teeth of these stupefying odds it is you and I, in our ordinariness, that are here.'

I think this captures my attitude to life and death fairly well. The fact that we die is what makes life precious. We must make the most of our time because it is a limited resource.

I hope you have a long and comfortable life, Max. I hope if there is a God then it is listening to you and allows you to live longer, and if there isn't, I hope your cancer goes into remission or that you are otherwise able to be cured.

But if that doesn't happen, I think you should take comfort in 3 things:

1. You have some time left, and you should make the most of it. Whether you live for 12 months or 120 years, decide on a few things you want to do and try your darndest to do them.

2. You have had a positive effect on the people around you. It's pretty clear from the comments on this blog that lots of people love you, and that you have touched a lot of people. I think you can take pride and comfort in that.

3. You will not be forgotten. I certainly won't be forgetting your bravery and from the looks of things many others won't either. You have left a lasting impact on people's lives.

I'll be thinking of you
Mike

tinkerl on October 20, 2015 at 1:41 pm said:

Dear Max, i was really impressed by your blog. I think you may also like to read some of Carl Sagan's thoughts. 'It is far better to grasp the universe as it really is than to persist in delusion, however satisfying and reassuring'. He is one of my heroes from being a child and since I am not blessed with the ability to express my thoughts (unlike yourself) I thought you may like to add him to your ideas.

Sally Glenn on November 2, 2015 at 7:27 pm said:

A truly incredible blog Max! What an outstanding way you have with words; words, of course, are revolutionary themselves (at least that is what all English teachers believe!). You are an inspiration to all your peers and teachers on so many levels. Miss Glenn

The Anonymous Revolutionary on November 2, 2015 at 7:45 pm said:

Thank you so much and I'm really glad you like the blog! – I'll try to keep analysing chapters from Tess. She was quite revolutionary in some ways.

– Max

31. CAPITALISM'S EVOLUTIONARY PHASES

Posted on October 17, 2015

I'll start by saying that this entry may be quite dense. The purpose of writing it is to explain and convey an understanding I've developed of how capitalism has adapted to survive over the years, a question I've been considering for a while now. I suppose you could call the ideas proposed here a theory (if I was to name it, I'd call it the Theory of Three Ages), and that's all it'll be for the moment; any advancement of this idea will only follow a lot of research on my part.

But, given that this is me explaining my ideas so far, I'll hopefully give you a good description of these three ages, and of how I believe exploitation has evolved over time. To do this, however, everyone needs to know what we're dealing with, so I'll start by asking you the following question:

What is capitalism?

It's often seen as the embodiment of free trade and economic liberties as opposed to state control. Because of the challenge Communism presented in the twentieth century, it would also be easy to cite capitalism as simply one of two political and economic currents in the world, and, after various failures in the Communist countries, it's far too often associated with freedom and harmony. Predictably, I'm going to tell you that this is wrong: it's the single most sly, destructive, exploitative concept that has dominated the world throughout modern history.

So here's a Marxist appraisal of our great nemesis.

The European Age

In terms of where it all began, capitalism arose roughly three centuries ago, taking its first breath in Italy. I wrote a more detailed entry on its origins a few months ago, but I'll cover the basics here. The system that takes precedence over all inhabitable continents is a relatively recent one; it developed in Europe, perhaps the most socially advanced corner of the Earth at that point, out of the decaying feudal system that formerly retained supremacy. Yet unlike feudalism, capitalism existed to provide industrial (as opposed to agricultural) production, and with its rise, the focus of the economy was no longer upon the farms, but the factories.

The European countries soon grew in power and influence, and rose to colonise great swathes of Africa, America,

Asia and Oceania, allowing them to exploit imperialistically. Imperialism has crept its way into history throughout mankind's many different epochs, and it has always been a tendency of the strongest individuals to dominate the weak – this can be viewed as the rise of capitalist imperialism. The new European empires sought to utilise the people and the resources of the colonised nations for capitalistic purposes, and thus expanded their field of economic influence to the far corners of the Earth.

These powers were thus able to sustain dominance, by widening their field of exploitation beyond national limits, yet it couldn't continue for ever. You could perhaps think of this period as the climax of capitalism, at which point exploitation had advanced humanity greatly, but had reached a critical level and was growing ever harder to maintain. Even after the establishment of a vast imperial network, the ruling elites of Britain, France and Germany were struggling to control those whose labour they relied upon. The system was, quite literally, falling apart under the weight of its own contradictions.

The American Age

Three significant changes took place in the world during the twentieth century. Firstly, the rise in power and influence of another giant, the United States, changed the international dynamic of the capitalist world. Secondly, economic changes allowed exploitation to take place to a less severe extent in the western countries, allowing many concessions to be made to the working population, and causing the working class to actually decline. Finally, the rise of Bolshevism threatened to end capitalism altogether.

It may not seems as though these changes could benefit capitalism, but, with the economic system on the very verge of collapse, they perhaps managed to save it.

The fact that the western countries found a common enemy in Soviet Russia and, later, China, Eastern Europe, Cuba and Communist Indochina contributed to this; they were forced to unite against

them. This can be seen most clearly in the Cold War, but was also evident prior to 1945. It demonstrates the development of a capitalist ideology, through the willingness of these nations to fight for motives like democracy and human rights (it is, in a Marxist sense, the tendency of capitalism to allow for greater political freedom) under the new guidance of the United States. It was then a question of whether or not the western proletariat would side with the Communist world, or the world run by their employers, and this sense of ideological unity helped allow for the latter. Tales of failures, inefficiencies and abuses in the socialist countries helped strengthen this ideology, and helped keep the workers from revolting, temporarily keeping them occupied and holding capitalism in place for longer.

Yet whilst ideological control helped distract many, the economic contradictions in the capitalist system were still such that it could not continue, and immediate reorganisation of the economy was needed if it were to do so. Economic variation took place in the form of de-industrialisation, causing the working class to shrink in size, and in the outsourcing of industry to other parts of the world. This gave rise to a new form of international domination, where brands and corporations, as opposed to armies and governments, became responsible for the unofficial and shadowy exploitation of the third world. Imperialism in the traditional sense, the official establishment of foreign authority in the region, was on the decline, again very much in tune with the tendency of capitalist society to progress in the direction of liberty and freedom, yet a new form of imperialism was developing. It was purely economic, and dodged the need for a military invasion and the controversy that such invasion causes, and yet it was more effective, and could allow the western proletariat to both decline and grow in affluence. They would thus lose their revolutionary character, and so capitalism was kept alive in the developed world.

In this way, an interesting dynamic fell into place, where the capitalist world, led by the United States, relied upon the undeveloped regions for economic purposes, and the Communist world, led by the Soviet Union, wished to bring an end to such western domination. This gave way to Third-World Marxism, a tendency in Communist thought influenced largely by Mao's teachings, which is still popular today. It may also be no coincidence that, outside the

Communist bloc, all the new revolutions occurred in undeveloped areas of the planet.

The International Age

Throughout the 1980s and '90s, the Communist empire fragmented and the majority of socialist states gave way to a shifting political climate, allowing capitalism to expand across Eurasia, consuming Russia, Eastern Europe and Central Asia. This led to further changes in the international dynamic, and paved the way for a future in which the United States may not be the leading capitalist power. As some of the still officially Communist countries resorted to capitalism, the rise of China presented a further challenge to the United States.

At the same time, the third world, which the capitalist world had become increasingly reliant upon, was developing at an astonishing rate. India, Brazil and Indonesia, whilst locked in the depths of poverty, all have the potential to become superpowers, which suggests that soon our imperial ventures in these parts of the world may no longer be tolerated. If this is to be the case, and even if not (as no format of capitalism can continue indefinitely) the capitalist world will do what it has done for decades, and scour the Earth for pockets of resources and workers to exploit. New pockets of exploitation have already opened up, in countries like Russia, the perfect example of economic polarisation, and more will likely appear as further geopolitical changes take place.

This, it seems, is the kind of capitalism we've adopted. In the European Age, exploitation took place within the confines of individual countries, with certain countries exercising capitalistic rule over others. In the American Age, the division between the exploited and the exploiters began to take on national characteristics, yet now, in the age of international economics, such divisions exceed these boundaries and exist irrespective of states and countries.

Revolution, whenever and wherever it occurs, must take place on an international level to compete with this system. Even though he was famously sparse on the practicalities of revolution, Karl Marx did remark that, whilst the differences between nations and nationalities are vanishing in a capitalistic society, 'the supremacy of the proletariat will cause them to vanish still faster'.

Today, as capitalism grows increasingly globalised, this couldn't be more relevant.

Janet Williamson on October 17, 2015 at 4:56 pm said:

HI Max – a very interesting piece! I would agree that we are now in an international age of capitalism in which the wealth and power of corporations can dwarf and challenge that of nation states, thus rendering capitalism ever harder to control. In this context I am particularly interested in your conclusion that revolution must be international to succeed, which I think raises some interesting questions about the role of the state. In the short term it is often governments who have the best chance of standing up to corporate power, especially if they act together and for that reason it seems right to try to strengthen the power of governments vis a vis corporations or at least demand of governments that they do not hand more power over to corporations through eg the Investor-State Dispute Settlements system in TTIP. But stronger national governments would arguably make revolution on an international level harder to achieve, rather than easier.

In part this goes back to the extent to which one believes that anything progressive can be achieved through the state within the capitalist system. I am more optimistic about this than you (remembering your blog about Corbyn) – looking at countries such as those of Scandinavia that are undoubtedly capitalist but in which there is a very different contract between the state, the working class and the capitalist class which generates much better outcomes for society, makes me believe that there are real gains to be achieved through government policy while still confined by the capitalist system. But another way of looking at the same thing is that I do not see the opportunities for revolution, whether national or international, at the moment, so see the best route to progressive change is working to reform the system we have. Perhaps you see more opportunities for revolution than I do currently; I would be very interested to see a future blog on that if that is the case!

Keep up the fight! All best, Janet (friend of Helen's)

The Anonymous Revolutionary on October 17, 2015 at 5:12 pm said:

I really like your ideas and agree that governmental control/ intervention does have some benefits to offer in the way of curbing international exploitation, but, as I believe revolution is the ultimate solution, I'd be very cautious about settling for less, as actions like state intervention are forms of compromise; this may make them counter-productive to the organisation of a revolutionary struggle. I'll try and post a future entry covering these ideas!

Max

Rachel on October 17, 2015 at 9:09 pm said:

This was so interesting to read, thanks Max!

Dai Hard on October 17, 2015 at 10:22 pm said:

How many of these emerging giants may yet go on to exert (cultural) imperialist tendencies themselves? What might the fourth age look like?

Yorkafka on October 18, 2015 at 7:05 am said:

Re 'The Fourth Age': how long before corporations (and not governments) become the de facto nation state, performing administrative functions at home and abroad? Walmart and McDonalds number 4 million employees between them & are growing at an alarming rate – McD's workforce has been increasing by 20,000 employees each and every year for the past decade. In 'hostile' environments (i.e. where some or all of the local population are not sympathetic to their aims) it is customary for western contractors to recruit their own 'private security' (armies in all but name) rather than rely upon the local government for protection. Of course this is no different to the behaviour of, say, the British East India Company 150-200 years ago, but the global reach of corporations today is vastly greater.

The Anonymous Revolutionary on October 18, 2015 at 7:11 am said:

I've thought about that – when the day will come when corporations take over the roles of governments. I think that if it happens, it'll happen sooner than most would imagine.

Liz Withyman on October 22, 2015 at 3:03 pm said:

Max,
This is my second attempt at replying to your latest blog entry – the first one seemed to disappear into the ether but being technically challenged as I am it may be that I'm not looking for it in the right place! So forgive the repetition if it turns up.

Your informative essay on Capitalism's Evolutionary Phases is another erudite piece of writing, complex and packed with detail. It is as you say 'dense' – too dense for me, or rather I'm too dense for it…

I accept the proposition that capitalism is unsustainable – the ever increasing rate of consumption which follows from capitalism, in the context of a planet with finite resources (and particularly a finite supply of oil which fuels the capitalist machine), as you say cannot continue indefinitely. A form of change is inevitable. What I find tricky is what should replace it, or how it should change…is true equality possible? Is it desirable?

On that topic, I have found a TED talk (I am a great fan of TED talks) you might enjoy called 'Capitalism Hits the Fan' by Prof Richard Wolff. As in my previous reply, sorry I don't know how to do links yet...

Keep up the good work with your blog – it is most inspiring. All in the Withyman household send their love xxxxx

Sue Littlemore on October 22, 2015 at 3:39 pm said:

Dear Max

I enjoyed your blog and you are so right that, for many people capitalism does not deliver freedom nor harmony.

A question to consider, therefore, is why do so many people just put up with it? Why no mass revolutionary uprising as Marx expected?

Perhaps we can look to the Middle East for clues to answer this – it seems the Arab Spring type uprisings in Egypt and Syria were cruelly suppressed by those whose interests are vested in the status quo. But what makes the difference between a mass protest which fails and one that works?

UK protests did overturn the poll tax. Miners' strikes failed to change energy policy.

To use a parochial example, I often wonder why so called consumer power and so called market competition fail to deliver for customers – we all hate call centres and long for the days when it was at least possible to speak to informed people who didn't read from scripts – but we have accepted this change.

Tonight I am going to a talk by Arnie Graf

who coached Barack Obama on how to support community activists trying to bring about change and is an expert on community campaigns.

I shall report back.

I send my very best wishes

Sue

Shalini on October 22, 2015 at 9:01 pm said:

Hi Max – Thank you for broadening my knowledge on capitalism. Great writing!

Nyx on October 23, 2015 at 6:59 am said:

You write so brilliantly. And put across your ideas so beautifully. But I still disagree with you. Capitalism, for all its many many faults, is here to stay. There will be no massive revolution. Nope. This is because capitalism fits with human nature. We humans are extraordinary and capable of the tremendous BUT are inherently selfish, not equal, lazy, looking out for ourselves… we like fun, stuff, comfort, beauty, home, nice things (bet even cavemen had massive cave envy) and we are ultimately driven by this deep down… Socialism is obviously a far far nobler, kinder, fairer, better system but we humans are too shabby and greedy to live like that. What I hope for the future is that we humans can increasingly globally join together… communicate… and temper the shabbiness. Grow up. Behave. Share. But as usual, until we are forced to change (i.e. really start to run out of resources, polar caps melt) we probably won't.

The Anonymous Revolutionary on October 23, 2015 at 10:12 am said:

Karl Marx disagrees! I understand why you might take that view, but it contradicts the Marxist belief that mankind isn't selfish or greedy by nature; these, as societal tendencies, are learned characteristics during human society's evolution. In early history, our civilisations were based on collective ownership and equality (an example would be the early Christian communes). Marx called this Primitive Communism. The selfishness that has defined our economic and political systems since only came about as a result of stronger individuals dominating weaker ones, capitalism being the most advanced format of such domination. I believe that man is now intelligent enough to realise the goal of a socialist society once again. This goal obviously clashes with the interests of the exploitative classes, which is why revolution is necessary. It may be the case that this revolution only occurs when the ice caps melt or we run out of crude oil reserves (times when change must be forced), but equality will still be the endgame, which isn't impossible; it's a return to our original state of being.

Nyx on October 23, 2015 at 3:35 pm said:

Well I disagree with Karl Marx!

Us humans ARE by nature selfish and greedy.

I was very interested when you wrote that 'in early history our civilisations were based on collective ownership and equality'. Really? Me, I'm struggling to think of anything much beyond hunter gatherers (that was a voluntary not compulsory set up though surely? 'OK guys, I'll go with Ugg here and bash an elk on the head, Arf... you stay behind and help hack it up later and oh can you sort the fire? The rest of you... look busy and guard the huts... then we'll all eat. That OK? Deal? Etc) but helpfully you gave me a proper sensible example... 'early Christian communes'... Ah I didn't know about them. Right OK I'll go look that up. Couldn't find much though. Where is your evidence for this? Bit of very v early church communal living in Jerusalem I can see... hmm...Though looks to me that a mutual sharing of possessions was simply best course of action to help get the early church going? Then they all the chaos left after a few months to spread the good word. Hardly a 'civilisation' and in fact as I casually googled away I was warned, together with the Thessalonians, by Paul that 'if a man will not work, he shall not eat'; 'earn the bread you eat' 2 Thess 3:10. That's not very socialist.

Then I remembered vaguely and at last found a story which sums up my views on Marx and his teachings and my fear that us humans ain't up to it. You v probably already know this tale but just in case.

William Bradford was the leader of a small band of separatists who founded the Plymouth Colony in Massachusetts in 1620. Times were harsh and half of the colony population died during the first nasty winter. Still, the pilgrims clung together and held their farmland communally. They divided their food, work and provisions fairly and evenly (yep all sounds good huh?) but before long, conflicts arose. Some of the lazier members started to take advantage of the harder working. The harder working members grew more and more resentful, frustrated and less and less productive… and everything fell apart. Bam. End of colony. Didn't work. Never does.

Primitive Communism? What does that mean? Tell me. But we are no longer primitive. Are you (and Marx) suggesting we somehow go back in time and collectively forget all that we now know? How can any sort of primitive lifestyle or in fact primitive anything be relevant now?

Capitalism adapts and changes and evolves and will survive. I think Marx overlooked capitalism's ability to change and adapt.

So? Over to you. Am braced for a shredding (albeit elegantly written) by you…

luke carroll on October 23, 2015 at 8:15 pm said:

Hi Max,
I enjoyed reading this piece and I think it provides some interesting arguments about the implications of global capitalism on the position of the proletariat. On the subject of global revolution and

how it can be achieved I think Gramsci's concept 'counter-hegemony' could provide an interesting approach. The global nature of capitalism requires a higher degree of interconnections between separate cultures, so as to manage a global economy. I think that this works to develop a global culture of sorts, in which the proletariat of different nations have greater means to interact than ever before and this leads to a greater degree of class consciousness; examples being the global justice movement and even the peer to peer nature of internet communications i.e. such as receiving news from independent journalists. The effects of this increasingly global culture is that it provides a more structured area in which the ideas of a counter-hegemony can grow and influence global civil society. If we view the relationship between the base and the super-structure as organistic then the global culture may provide the means for a global revolution, following the establishment of an international counter-hegemony. Ironically a counter-hegemonic global culture would be able to utilise the institutional framework provided by advanced capitalism to bring about its ruin. I'd be interested to see your thoughts on whether a global revolution would take this form; or whether other measures would be necessary to overthrow capitalism.

Luke

The Anonymous Revolutionary on October 24, 2015 at 7:10 pm said:

That's a really interesting idea. I hadn't thought about that, but the internationalisation of capitalism would allow workers worldwide to develop an independent culture, so I agree that revolutionaries can use this to their advantage.

32. FIVE CANDIDATES FOR FUTURE REVOLUTION

Posted on October 23, 2015

Capitalism today is not capitalism as Marx described it, over a century ago, and our economic system is the product of much evolutionary change relating to the political and financial situations in the nineteenth, twentieth and twenty-first centuries. Now in a new age of economic exploitation (I wrote a lot more about this in my previous entry), the antagonisms between the bourgeoisie and the proletariat have changed character once more, and thus, revolutionary potential can be seen in several areas of the world that could have been glossed over by the Marxist intellectuals/ Communist movement several years ago.

Here's a list I made of five countries (in no particular order) which, I believe, will make the best candidates for future proletarian revolution. The countries are judged on two things: which would be the most likely, and which would be the most strategically beneficial, in the name of advancing Communism and spreading the revolution worldwide. There's also an element of wishful thinking, hence the inclusion of the UK, where I live, when other countries would probably have equal claim to that position (although in fairness, I was trying to keep it to five!) Feel free to comment and add to the list, and remember, this isn't a complete assessment; it's only representative of how I view the world today.

1. United Kingdom

A dwindling, yet still hugely prominent power in the western world, Britain contributes greatly to the network of international capitalism. From the industries of Wales, Scotland and the larger British cities, to the overseas resources harvested by British companies, the signs of exploitation are clear. It's also telling that many are surprised at the rigidity and profoundness of the UK's class system, which still resembles that of an old capitalist power, despite the complicating effects of capitalism's internationalisation. For example, it may surprise you that in 1996, a UN report revealed Britain to be the most unequal country in the western world, and a recent report (http://www.independent.co.uk/news/uk/politics/report-finds-that-britains-wages-are-the-most-unequal-in-europe-10259077.html) shows that the country's wages are the most unequal in the EU.

There are those who argue that revolution isn't possible in first-world countries like the UK, but this isn't true. What is certainly apparent is that the country's working class has shrunk and living/working standards have improved as the country has grown more reliant on foreign exploitation. However contemporary studies of our class system still reveal a large percentage of exploited individuals with a potentially rebellious character (evidence: the London and Birmingham riots of 2011) and furthermore, the hoards of foreign workers who constitute a large percentage of Britain's workforce should not be excluded from the revolution. If a Communist movement was to take power, it should act on behalf of these people, and embrace their revolutionary potential. Should this occur, it would serve as a nail in the heart of the capitalist web.

2. Greece

The birthplace of Plato, Aristotle and Ptolemy started to demonstrate significant potential for change after the financial crisis of 2007–8. One of the hardest-hit countries in Europe, Greece has already shown signs of future revolutionary activity by the radicalisation of its national politics. Recently, a former Communist was voted into power, showing not only the shift in views to extremes (something common in revolutionary situations), but a significant shift to the left. A neo-Nazi party with a fantastically sinister name (Golden Dawn) also did worryingly well in the recent election of early 2015, which tells us too how desperate their situation is.

If real change were to happen as a result of such desperation, we might see something of a reignition in the Balkans. Greece, unlike Bulgaria, Hungary or Yugoslavia, has never experienced Communism, yet if fresh revolution were to establish a socialist Greek republic, it could spread and advance beyond the borders with Albania and Bulgaria, spurring revolutions across the whole of crisis-ridden Europe.

3. China (#2)

The revolutionary Maoist state is now one of the most exploitative and ruthlessly capitalistic nations on the planet. What began with reform and relaxation of Communist policy resulted in the counter-revolutionary reintroduction of industrial exploitation, to the extent that the western powers now thrive on Chinese production, because they can get away with worse than they could at home. It's time for the Chinese proletariat to realise they live under a pretence of a socialism, the reality being anything but. It's time for a second 1949.

Not only would this be a highly valuable victory on the road to world revolution, given the huge potential China offers in the way of building and advancing Communism, but it would help change the worldwide perception of the former. Today, many people with little knowledge of Marxism may happily take the view that China is a Communist country. After all, it's ruled by the Chinese Communist Party, it bears a red flag, and it's officially known as the People's Republic of China. But a second Chinese revolution will help to change this, and will hopefully allow people to appreciate the difference between genuine equality and masked exploitation.

4. India

India has, for centuries, been victimised by capitalism. Ever since the United Kingdom colonised the country, it was subject to imperialist exploitation in the interests of its colonists. Since the departure of the British, India has been victimised by a new form of imperialism, with workers in sweatshops sewing clothes for western companies, their consumers in France, Britain and the United States happy to turn a blind eye. Now, the country is quickly rising as an advanced, capitalist power – yet the majority of its citizens live under the yoke of capitalism, impoverished by inequality.

Revolution in India would change the lives of over a billion people, and would transform the political landscape of South Asia, given the immense size and influence of the country. An advanced nuclear power with a space agency, one of the largest armies on the planet and a culture famous throughout the world, this country's importance is obvious. In addition to this, a strong Communist movement already exists in the country. I part from them ideologically as they are largely influenced by Maoism, but their presence nonetheless shows something remarkable: a people fighting back.

5. Russia (#2)

Russia existed for seventy-four years under Communist rule, a world record in that regard. The collapse of the Soviet Union in 1991, however, saw the national economy diverge, giving rise to both wealth and poverty in extremes. The oligarchy that now owns much of Siberia's oil exists at the expense of many deprived citizens. According to Tim Marcin's article on the ibtimes, the number of Russians living in poverty has topped twenty-two million (http://www.ibtimes.com/russia-poverty-critical-amid-western-sanctions-oil-price-dropping-2008577).

Putin has tried to fill the void left by the fall of Communism by cultivating nationalism, but I don't believe this solution will last in a country like this, with an economy driven by business elites, likely with government connections. A return of Bolshevism will also hopefully end the attitude of strict conservatism fuelled by the Eastern Orthodox Church, and I don't know, but it seems right that when it comes to building socialism, seventy years of experience should make a difference. Lenin, the original founder of Communist Russia, once said that 'It is impossible to predict the time and progress of revolution', nonetheless, I believe we can count this country a likely candidate for the next one.

Yorkafka on October 23, 2015 at 10:07 pm said:

Can we please add Yorkshire to the list?

kimemiamaina on October 24, 2015 at 8:28 am said:

Or Swaziland, with its redundant constitutional monarchy, or Kenya where rampant corruption, and skyrocketing interest rates are squeezing the population, or Brazil, or Palestine.
   Basically did you take a good look at the 'Global South' at all before writing this?

The Anonymous Revolutionary on October 24, 2015 at 10:44 am said:

If Kenya, Swaziland or Palestine turned Communist the global impact would be minimal, so, whilst revolution may be likely in countries like these, they'd only fulfil my first criteria. Revolution in a country like Brazil may have a larger impact, but I was trying to limit the list to five.

Ruthie on October 25, 2015 at 6:53 pm said:

When considering the possibility of revolution you should also consider the culture and history of a country. The UK has never had a revolution and I don't believe British society would support a revolution. There is the possibility of radical change via democratic means. If you haven't read it you should read 'A Very British Coup' https://en.wikipedia.org/wiki/A_Very_British_Coup
    It describes the election of a left wing PM with views not dissimilar to Jeremy Corbyn's. Could it happen?

Russ on October 25, 2015 at 7:32 pm said:

Another really interesting article to read.
    The UK has been pretty stable since Charles I... Perhaps it will take a lot more than two terms of

a regressive government to see a change of this magnitude? But to see a serious improvement in equality of opportunity would be something indeed. Labour tried and failed to meaningfully alter in the last economic cycle when they had the chance.

Hang in there anonymous revolutionary.

Dan Medina on October 27, 2015 at 11:36 am said:

I would like to know your take on quantitative easing and the reality of negative interest rates.
Best Dan

Chris Grayling on October 27, 2015 at 5:27 pm said:

Hello Max
Your aunt told me about your blog and about your situation. I'm clearly not quite in the same place as you ideologically, but you make some interesting arguments, and I just wanted to wish you all the very best at what must be a really difficult time. You are very brave.

Best wishes
Chris Grayling MP
Leader of the House of Commons.

33. 'NATURALLY SELFISH': DOES HUMAN NATURE MAKE SOCIALISM IMPOSSIBLE?

Posted on October 30, 2015

When discussing socialism, hearing others discuss socialism and looking at the various pro/con arguments on the topic, I've come across several ideas as to why Communism is a flawed system, why there will never be a revolution and why, at the end of the day, we're better off how we are. Some cite certain atrocities in various Communist countries and draw a conclusion about their inevitable presence in such a system, whereas others will simply tell you that it's an unrealistic goal which will never be achieved in the real world. There are also those who will object on moral grounds, defending their right to private ownership, but perhaps the most interesting proposition I've come across is the idea that Communism is rendered unachievable by human nature itself.

I can understand how this argument would appeal to many, as it seems to make logical sense; humans have a long-standing tendency towards selfishness. This can be seen in both a social and a biological manner, with mankind's survival being based on Darwinian principles, and its prosperity on socially Darwinian ones. It would appear that competition is both an innate and necessary component of human wellbeing, which suggests that building a collective society based on the principles of equality is impossible. I'm going to argue the opposite, or, more importantly, I'm going to approach the issue from a Marxist perspective.

In Marx's eyes, mankind has progressed through various historical epochs, each based on the dominant economic class in the era, which has managed to control and utilise the means of production for its own gain. So far, we have seen society progress from slavery to feudalism, and later, to capitalism. Regardless of your views regarding Marxism generally, a study of global history tells us that this progression is more or less accurate, and it provides a solid basis for historical analysis in this case.

Each of the epochs described here are based on the principles of inequality and exploitation, but there is, in fact, an earlier stage in this model of human development, referred to by Marx as Primitive Communism. These were the days of man's tribal history, when hunter-gatherer societies roamed the planet, and when socialism was the accepted norm. The tribes man formed in the ancient world exemplify society devoid of exploitation, or in other words, a Communist lifestyle, which totally defies the judgement of those who claim this isn't possible.

Several indigenous peoples like these have survived in the present era, such as the Penan people of Borneo, who live according to the principles of equality, have no actual leaders (only spokespeople who wield no power) and are known for practising 'molong' (never taking more than is necessary). The Adi people of India and the Maasai tribe of East Africa are also provide examples of preserved tribal socialism, and Israeli kibbutzim, alongside various anarchist communities today, represent successful attempts to recreate this lifestyle in the modern world. They remind us that our condition in the past is not reflective of that of today.

Maasai tribesmen

It's also telling that this was our earliest state of being, and the fact that our first and most basic attempts at civilisation were not based on greed or self-indulgence (rather the reverse) shows that not only are selflessness and collective organisation possible, but they are natural to mankind. Only after individuals took over the productive means did the focus shift to individual rather than communal gain, meaning economic exploitation and unequal distribution are learned habits. This argument is further supported by the fact that humanity is still struggling to find happiness, no matter how much wealth we accumulate. Statistics on contentment or satisfaction in developed countries demonstrate this, proving that endless buying and spending do not make us any happier, and suggesting that it is not an innate desire to strive for one's own gain at the expense of others. Needless to say, this kind of consumption is also incredibly unsustainable, meaning that, like it or not, capitalism must give way to a better economic system.

Coming back to Darwinism, I understand that societal competition is not natural to mankind, the argument seems to contradict the competitive biological nature of mankind's development, based on the principle of survival of the fittest. However, it may surprise the non-Marxist that Marx was a great admirer of Darwin's, and saw his ideas on the evolution of organisms, through the process of natural selection, to be at one with his own ideas regarding society's evolution, through the process of class struggle. It isn't necessarily counter-evolutionary that humanity's natural state is a collective one; it has merely evolved from this condition in the same way that cells and organisms repeatedly do, and nor does the belief that man will 'return' to socialism contradict the ideas of competitive evolution, for, with the rise of Communism, we are simply seeing the end of an evolutionary process. In a way, we're seeing something similar in the natural world today; survival of the fittest has determined humanity's evolution since its birth, yet with advances in the medical sciences, we're now able to preserve 'unfit' characteristics and curb natural selection. Should this continue in the future, humanity may never need to adapt, and evolution would no longer occur.

This is why I believe that human nature does not contradict equality, but rather allows for it. True, we have a tendency to put our own needs above those of others, but at the end of the day, our earliest efforts at working together show that these unhealthy behaviours aren't innate or fixed, even if they fuel the exploitative economic systems of modern society. In a debate on the benefit and rationality of religion, I once heard it remarked that, unlike squids, which apparently spend almost their entire lives in isolation, humans are social creatures. However unsociable capitalist society may make us seem, I believe this is certainly something to remember.

Yorkafka on October 30, 2015 at 10:45 pm said:

Great post! Down with the squids – you listening Mr Grayling? Engels once wrote: 'The middle classes have a truly extraordinary conception of society. They really believe that human beings … have real existence only if they make money or help to make it.'

Mind you, he also said 'If there were no Frenchwomen, life wouldn't be worth living' (but then we all have off days).

Except you it would appear. Well done Mr Anonymous Revolutionary!

Helen Kent on November 2, 2015 at 12:35 pm said:

A very thought provoking post – my favourite so far.

It had me reading up on the tribes you mentioned and considering the pros and cons of past and present collective lifestyles. Like you I'm pleased to find ancestors whose existence wasn't based on 'greed and self-indulgence', though I am not sure this is humankind's 'natural' state.

It could be argued that living collectively was due to necessity (a single hunter/gatherer wouldn't get very far) and that a prerequisite is having vast amounts of space to hunt/gather in. When the land could support everyone (and belong to no one) it was, perhaps, easier for humans to share.

The environmental argument for a more collective and sustainable life-style is a strong one. I didn't know about (& now admire) the Penan's practice of 'molong' (never taking more than is necessary). If Wikipedia can be trusted then the Penan also don't have a word for 'thank you', as 'help is assumed and therefore doesn't require thanks'. According to Survival International the Penan are in desperate need of help themselves and your blog indirectly led to me donating to a campaign to highlight their plight. If others are similarly moved and interested they might want to read more here:

http://www.survivalinternational.org/tribes/penan

Nyx on November 2, 2015 at 2:47 pm said:

Your writing stuns me. So beautiful. All woven together so cleverly… neatly. Me though, I always struggle to find the words that I need especially now that I'm trying to post here… staring up at your skills. But I am going to try because I have to tell you… and I never thought that this would happen… but I think you are shifting and changing my views on Marx, socialism… capitalism… the future… and I have thought so much about what you've said… here and in your previous posts.

Was watching a clip from Star Trek at the weekend

(bear with). Kirk and the gang, all used to a life in the 24th century, suddenly find themselves in, and baffled by, a present day (well OK the 1980s) San Francisco. They try and fail to board a mini bus: 'We need to get money!' exclaims Kirk. 'They still use money!!' Yes yes yes I know it's just Star Trek but it made me think about your blog. And the future.

Because I do agree with you that our present economic situation IS unsustainable… we WILL be forced to, amongst other things, find a new store of value, medium of exchange and I certainly hope by the 24th century we will have got there. A new world system WILL have to evolve. Capitalism and socialism… can't believe they'll even exist as distinct ideologies then? Do you? Everything is going to change and that is obviously the only certainty.

But ooof I do hope for a sartorially better future than Star Trek would have us imagine; please dear God no nasty tunics, velcro and badly cut trousers etc. Though a jump suit CAN look good with the right heels… OK enough from me.

The Anonymous Revolutionary on November 3, 2015 at 9:04 pm said:

Thanks so much – you can take some credit as the blog post was inspired by your comments. I think that by the twenty-fourth century capitalism will have been replaced by a sustainable, redistributive system (socialism), but whether socialism or capitalism will exist as ideologies, or even words, I suppose we'll never know. Either way, I think we can hope for something better than Kirk's world!

Nyx on November 5, 2015 at 6:21 pm said:

Heavens no… it is I who have to thank YOU! Feels like you have reached in and given my brain a good ol' shake.

Let's not diss Kirk's 24th cent world too much though. Muscle past the unsophisticated use of primary colour blocking in clothing and you can sense that there IS equality, tolerance, fairness and general harmony with, now that I think about it, very little sign of any crazed consumerism. Plus the doors make lovely swishy noises and hey, teleportation! Come on that would be fun.

Karen on November 3, 2015 at 12:39 am said:

Hi Max,
Really liked this post. You should also look at models such as Norway which at least appears to be socialist in nature. They had a similar amount

of oil as Britain once did. They ensured that the oil was owned by the people and so the profits were distributed to society. The money from the sale of oil was reinvested into finding green energy (Norway is almost entirely green energy now) and providing the people in Norway with all the things they needed, good roads, transport, leisure time, health care. In essence it filled the public purse to bursting point so that the whole of society benefited. By contrast Britain allowed the vast majority of its similar oil reserves to be owned by individuals and companies, the profits were therefore distributed to the rich only with nothing to show for this. In Norway the profits from the oil industry are still public money and reinvested into society in Norway only now most of the oil is sold to other countries as Norway needs very little of it. Norway recently put a tax on overtime of something like 70% as they were of the view that the people did not need more money, that overtime was unproductive and that this time was better spent with family and friends. As a nation they are much more inclined to share ideas and seek out sensible solutions which benefit all rather than seeking out what will produce the most profit. The politicians are all sensible and boring, picked for their skills for the job. The royal family live in normal homes in the city and travel by public transport. As a society they believe in rehabilitating offenders back into society, on the basis that they believe that this will in the long term benefit the person and will be better for society than paying to keep them in prison for life. The prisons are all rehabilitative open plan with therapy at its heart. This is the case for every offender even those who committed the most appalling crimes.

The world is waking up to the terribly damaging effects of consumerisim. There is an interesting movement called the circular economy. Idea is to design all products to be dissembled and the bi-products used elsewhere. In order for this to work properly no one would own products they would lease them, once done with rather than throw them away they return them to the manufacturers who then dissembles them and either use the remains themselves to build the newer model or send them to another company to use for another product. Moving away from the constant consumption of capitalism. For this movement to work it requires companies to work together with a mutual interest, it also requires a high degree of cooperation amongst the designers and producers and manufacturers, and to some extent the consumers who will have to give back their product and give up any sense of ownership. Pretty socialist idea.

This is also starting to happen in other areas such as housing with friends and family purchasing together or living in what is now referred to as urban communities. What started as a necessary way to afford to live in a property with space in large cities has proved to be much more with people reporting that they are happier sharing their homes, as this provides them with a sort of community or family where they share meals together and are company for one another, look after each others' things when the other is away on hols, help each other out etc etc.

I even think the likes of AirBnB have encouraged people to be more socialist, as people have to open their homes to strangers/foreigners. All for a mutual benefit. Someone's spare room not being wasted and someone else getting cheap accommodation and a real life experience of a country from the home of someone who lives there. The history of AirBnB is very interesting, it being started as a social experiment. However it has grown and people are enjoying having strangers in their home, sharing ideas and experiences with people who are from completely different religious, cultural and ethnic backgrounds.

In short I think as Bob Dylan said the times are a changin, even in all consuming Britain.

The Anonymous Revolutionary on November 3, 2015 at 9:09 pm said:

Thank you. These are all great examples of small-scale socialism – they make you more optimistic about humanity.

Rudolf on November 3, 2015 at 6:50 pm said:

A lovely read!
   If you are interested in Darwinism and competition, you might want to give Kropotkin's 'Mutual Aid: A factor of evolution' (1902) a go. Wikipedia summarises it well:
   'Written partly in response to social Darwinism and in particular to Thomas H. Huxley's Nineteenth Century essay, "The Struggle for Existence", Kropotkin's book drew on his experiences in scientific expeditions in Siberia to illustrate the phenomenon of cooperation. After examining the evidence of cooperation in nonhuman animals, in pre-feudal societies and medieval cities, and in modern times, he concluded that cooperation and mutual aid are the most important factors in the evolution of species and the ability to survive.'
   Here is a link to it, if you fancy a read: https://www.complementarycurrency.org/ccLibrary/Mutual_Aid-A_Factor_of_Evolution-Peter_Kropotkin.pdf

Jim Al-Khalili on November 4, 2015 at 4:00 pm said:

Hi Max. Just discovered your blog. A very eloquent and intelligently put case. I'll be following future blogs!
   Jim Al-Khalili

Gray Rabbitt on November 4, 2015 at 5:55 pm said:

A fine blog, Max. I don't think the 'Darwinian Competition' argument against Marxism is taken so seriously as it once was. A counter-argument is that cooperative and altruistic behaviour in social animals, like chimps and early us, is a strong drive to develop communication skills (e.g. language) and also a larger and more efficient brain to handle complexities of life in a social group. It pays to be cooperative and work for the benefit of the group because that is the best strategy for ensuring species survival.

But great stuff !

Sam on November 5, 2015 at 10:33 pm said:

Very interesting post, Max.

OK, here's my take on it. I get the fact that sharing is a natural instinct in humans and one that can still be adopted as a central or guiding principle for small groups (clubs, communes, even small societies or the indigenous groups you mention), which they can use in their day to day dealings with one another and with considerable benefit.

But my query is how it works in a geopolitical context. Can it work in larger societies, which, because of their size, tend to require the normal apparatus of state (i.e. government, rule of law, police etc.)? Once a society gets to a certain size, the only way that the principle of the sharing of resources can be 'enforced' above all others, given that the desire to share inevitably comes into conflict with other human emotions, is through a totalitarian state, i.e. extreme power wielded by the State. So the primitive Communism you refer to has a natural ceiling in effect.

That the end result is totalitarianism (which is generally accepted as being a bad thing) obviously has some precedent in history, but I suppose the question is this:

Is it (totalitarianism) an inevitable consequence of what I would simplistically label the natural conflict between human emotions such as greed (which is always going to happen), or is it not quite so fundamental in origin and instead the result of external influences or causes, which if it was possible to remove, would bring Marxists closer to their goals?

If so, the first step is to identify what those external influences or causes are that have derailed the project on the occasions it has been attempted in the last 100 years or so.

Just a thought – would be interested in your views!

34. REMEMBERING OCTOBER

Posted on November 6, 2015

Tonight, ninety-eight years to this day, the October Revolution occurred.

As (in my opinion) it was the most significant revolution, the most important event in the struggle against capitalism, and the greatest achievement of the international left, I decided to dedicate this entry to its anniversary…

Happy November 6th/7th comrades!

'The Bolshevik' – Boris Kustodiev

…Here's some light musical accompaniment:
https://youtu.be/_sxTbfeYdO0

Anwen on November 9, 2015 at 7:13 pm said:

I thought at first the beard was a little Lenin-like, but on reflection I think it's fuller…

chris on November 10, 2015 at 7:59 am said:

Hi Max,
Best anthem ever written by a million miles. Chris

35. THE EVILS OF INACTION: CAPITALISM AND THE MIGRANT CRISIS

Posted on November 13, 2015

With thousands of refugees hoping to be granted asylum in Europe, the continent has responded to the crisis with much resentment. Only recently did anti-migration demonstrators bearing neofascist slogans take to the streets of Warsaw, completely dwarfing the pro-migration rally that was taking place the same day. Their opinions are undoubtedly shared by many across Europe; as we have seen, it's not only ordinary citizens who are to blame; the use of tear gas and water cannons upon migrants at the Hungarian border shows government's outright hostility towards migrants, and the fact that according to Swedish opinion polls a far-Right, anti-immigration party is the country's most popular choice shows that mob mentality isn't just present on the streets.

In an attempt to at least respond to the event, the United Kingdom has agreed to accept a quota of 20,000 refugees. Even a relatively small contribution such as this was met with disdain, with many fearing for the stability of the nation after such an influx. It's evident that none of those talking of stability have ever lived in Syria.

One thing is clear: thousands are pouring into our wealthy, stable nations to escape war, poverty and discrimination, and it's as if we're doing everything we can to shut off the flow of people and put up our national boundaries. The refusal to accept quotas or the angst about allowing more citizens into one's country may be justified by a belief that Europe can't cope with the influx, or that we won't be able to provide for these people, yet these ideas are almost laughable if you compare the provisional capabilities of France, Britain or Poland with those of the dishevelled states these migrants are flocking from. When we finally realised that we couldn't ignore the issue, it was as though we reluctantly did as little as possible to get around it. Take the UK, for example. I firmly believe it could provide for many more than 20,000. Perhaps not without harming the grossly unequal hierarchy of wealth that dominates in Britain, but some sacrifice of wealth and resources is obviously needed. Unsurprisingly, the wealthy nations of the west are yet again unwilling to sacrifice theirs.

In this respect, the recent migrant crisis is part of a far larger problem, for it is well known, for example, that there is enough food in the world to feed everybody, yet some live in luxury while others starve. This reflects the economic disparity between nations of the first and third worlds, which remains a necessity for either's existence, and will always be preserved by wealthy countries simply by their refusal to change it, and jeopardise their affluence. This refusal to act, to utilise the economy for purposes that contradict their interests, is an inherent evil of the international bourgeoisie. Europe's refusal to take more responsibility is only a new manifestation of the same old problem; the unwillingness of the wealthy to change the status quo. We can only hope that, when such change doesn't come, there are enough voices out there to insist upon it.

Helen Kent on November 13, 2015 at 8:12 pm said:

Good post Max. I'm glad you've written about the migration/refugee crisis. When I first learnt of the Holocaust I couldn't understand why other countries didn't give visas to all the Jews desperate to escape. This feels similar – so many fleeing wars, poverty and persecution – and the response is to hope they will either stay put or go away.

Lucy Coles on November 13, 2015 at 11:07 pm said:

Very interesting, Max. Did you see the Daily Mail headlines – one saying basically 'stop them coming over here' and the next week, when that poor toddler was washed up on the shores of Greece, something like: 'Britain must open its door to refugees'.

fatherwilliams on November 13, 2015 at 11:41 pm said:

You may be the anonymous revolutionary, but if what you write is Marxism, then I am an accidental Marxist. I most certainly am a 'Maxist' and fully and whole-heartedly agree with all that you write. The failure to act by wealthy states like ours (Denmark, in my case) is a shame, and should be a crime. I read everything you write with great interest and admiration.

Yours sincerely, theaccidentalmarxist

Jacqueline Casey on November 14, 2015 at 12:21 am said:

Max, great human writing and analysis, I do not think it matters about ideology, Europe has acted like a spoilt petulant child for so long and has treated the developing and the undeveloped nations with such brutality that I think the people in Western nations could be deemed to be mentally unstable. I think that whatever form government takes, it should have an ethical foundation and that is lacking in the West and feeds into the global instability.

Jonas on November 14, 2015 at 4:19 pm said:

Greetings from the former 'Karl-Marx-Stadt', now known as Chemnitz, Germany. I have to say I agree with the gist of your post, but perhaps I may offer the German perception of events as an expansion of sorts. 'A touch of realism':

Every week we have demonstrations by the group known as 'PEGIDA' – I do not know how well known they are outside of our borders, their name means 'Patriotic Europeans Against the Islamisation of the Occidental World.' Without a shred of irony, the local branch of PEGIDA hold their weekly meetings at the world's second largest bust, the giant head of Karl Marx situated in the city centre. But in all their ignorance, they represent a rather small minority in this country. And that despite the fact that Germany has let in literally hundreds of thousands of refugees, indeed approaching one million.

So in a rather stark contrast to Great Britain, or most other European countries, we have actually taken your advice and gone with a policy of: 'Let in as many as possible'. And now we are discovering the side effects of that – and mild as they are for the moment, there are some significant problems looming on the horizon:

1) Every refugee needs to be registered and given a temporary or permanent visa. Then they need some form of financial assistance and some form of integrative assistance (such as an education program) and of course somewhere to actually live. All of these points require an enormous host of border-police, communal politicans, lawyers, doctors, bureaucrats of a dozen branches, etc. And we have simply reached the limit for how many people of those professions exist in Germany at the moment – the training of additional staff in all those fields is ongoing, but will not happen overnight.

2) There is a growing right wing movement against the influx of so many foreigners, as increasing parts of the population begin to fear radical changes in their surroundings. Of course you can I know those changes would mostly be beneficial – an additional Syrian fast food restaurant here, a couple more Syrian language schools there – but to a part of the population any change will always be bad change and they must be pandered to, in a way, by ensuring that change happens slowly enough for them to feel comfortable with it. Failing to pander to this gut feeling which many people seem to possess risks a right wing backlash, as is already occuring in many areas, with the bombing of

refugee camps and a general increase of violence.

3) Carrying on from point two, we have also experienced a growing left wing radicalisation in response to the growing right. I am aware that I am writing on a deeply left wing website, but from your posts I do not take you for a radical. The left wing radicals in Germany advocate the expulsion or physical suppression of the right wing – a move akin to quenching a fire by smothering it in oil. We are moving, as a country, towards a seriously dangerous rift in our society, a move which may in the near future cost a lot of lives.

Thus, as I said, merely a small expansion upon the views you have shared. People should share their wealth, share their living space, share whatever it is that other people do not possess and desperately need. But as we are beginning to see, it cannot be done without taking into consideration what the population feels, or has the capacity to do, about the situation. In Germany we are, in a way, blessed to have such horrific experiences in our history. It has made the entire population very careful about supporting reactionary movements, and very open to tolerance. As a German I feel it would be great if other countries shared the refugee load more evenly – but I wonder, at times, whether other countries would not break rather more quickly under such a load. Even if the economies, crime rates, religions of a country would be more or less unaffected (or affected positively in the case of the economy) by refugees, if the population does not approve (and does not approve to the point of becoming militant in voicing their disapproval) then perhaps it will not be possible to take in more people in future, and all idealist concepts to the contrary would end in rather dreadful conflicts.

chris on November 15, 2015 at 1:38 pm said:

Hi Max,

I've just been watching an 'expert' on Fox, the channel liberal Americans watch for its comedy value, talking in the light of the Paris atrocities. To let Syrian refugees into America, he says, is to condemn Americans to death in their own country. Among the innocent and dispossessed, he claims, there will be terrorists.

On March 16th, 1190 – and I guess you'll know more than most about this – around the same number of Jews were killed in York as people were killed in Paris 48 hours ago. So, nine hundred years on and still we find people who thought they were safe within their community being butchered. The pressure on Chancellor Merkel's refugee policy has just increased.

I commend the British Communist Party's response to the refugee crisis. The UK's appalling stance is rightly condemned, but the need for wealthy nation states to fund, support and trust the UN is also highlighted. Actually, I don't think Communist ideology and Charter principle are easily reconciled (monolithic world of Communist states versus a more politically diverse paradigm), but the call to get behind the UN resonates. Fund it properly, find its leaders from the brightest and best and let national interest assume a supporting role as we seek to resolve this dreadful situation.

36. PERPETUATING THE CYCLE OF VIOLENCE

Posted on November 21, 2015

The recent terror attacks in Paris have spurred much debate on terrorism, with many taking the view that action needs to be taken if we're to prevent anything like this from happening again. French president Hollande himself declared war on Islamic State, announcing plans to intensify airstrikes in the region, and he's not alone; British prime minister David Cameron also proposed British intervention in the area, and talk is now underway of an international coalition to fight ISIS militants. Yet how effective are these measures actually going to be?

It's worth remembering that Islamic State, whilst taking responsibility for these atrocities, announced that they were carried out in retaliation for France's recent actions in the Middle East. Thus, it seems bizarre that the country is choosing to respond to a disaster by committing more of the same actions that inspired it in the first place, especially since, as we are surely beginning to realise now, they don't work.

The western powers have organised countless attacks in this part of the world, destroying many innocent lives and communities in the name of stamping out terrorism, and, through the continuation of western social imperialism, have achieved nothing, for Islamic fundamentalism is just as pressing an issue as ever. In fact, I think we can say that

223

imperialism shares a large portion of the blame for the existence of these organisations in the first place; according to Pelp and Feldman's research, 95% of suicide attacks are the result of foreign occupation. Given this unsurprising trend, showing that aggressive military action in a foreign country will likely turn its citizens against yours, we can see that an increase in French airstrikes will only contribute to the already existing cycle of violence.

Yet whilst I'm surprised at their inability to see sense, I'm not surprised at the eagerness of France to resort to such violence, for this was the country that only recently helped to destroy the state of Libya, contributed to the violence in Mali, and, prior to the Paris attacks, backed US intervention in Syria and Lebanon. During these campaigns, and the many others carried out by the US-aligned nations, many atrocities occurred and many found themselves alienated from the western world, fuelling the bloodshed that took place last week in the French capital.

To wade deeper into the Syrian conflict, as Hollande has promised to do, will only add fuel to the fire.

Sarah Aspinall on November 23, 2015 at 9:28 am said:

Well said Max. I agree that we never seem to learn from history and that violence inevitably leads to more violence. I also agree that if we in the West collectively just slightly adjusted our expectations in regards to wealth/lifestyle, then there would be room for more compassionate response to the migrant crisis. But getting society as a whole to agree to this, as opposed to just imposing more restriction on the already-constrained (through benefit cuts etc), is a huge challenge. I find it difficult to imagine how we could achieve such a seismic change peaceably.

chris edwards on November 23, 2015 at 11:55 pm said:

Agree. Hollande's rhetoric after the atrocities was a carbon copy of post 9/11 Bush. I had hoped the lowest common denominator might be higher now.

Seemingly not. IS has created a magical space in a drab, once hopeless wasteland. Radical Jihadi ideology offers excitement, drama and, sometimes, victory. The 7th century is offering more than the 21st. We need to ask ourselves why that might be.

Post imperialist (sic) Middle East is now a complicated place. America once gave support to the 'green belt' of nations neighbouring or near Russia in the hope that a strong ring of Islamic states on Soviet borders might help weaken Communism. Now the PKK, PYD, YPG have the American support while being denounced by IS as 'Communist organisations'. The acme of US realpolitik I suppose.

Chris

Lucy Coles on November 28, 2015 at 8:29 pm said:

Bit late in commenting here but just thought you should know I found myself – after the Paris attacks – turning to your blog rather than the papers, because I knew you'd have something wise to say.

I completely agree. An eye for an eye is not the way forward.

37. WHO DO WE SIDE WITH? – ASSESSING RELATIONS IN A REVOLUTIONARY STRUGGLE

Posted on November 27, 2015

The issues regarding the practicalities of revolution have, for a long time, divided opinions within Communist circles. Karl Marx provided a theoretical basis for almost all things Marxist, from the alienation of the worker in capitalist society to the scientific progression of history, but this was one area which seems to have been glossed over, allowing the theorists and activists in his wake to devise individual interpretations. From this fresh wave of contributions to Marxist philosophy there arose Lenin's model of a Vanguard Party, Luxembourg's critique of Bolshevism in favour of revolutionary democracy and Pannekoek's concept of Council Communism, an idea which surfaced some years later in Tito's Yugoslavia.

One issue in particular, which spurred significant international debate in the years following the Russian Revolution, was that of association. Many Communists were prepared to work with other parties and organisations to advance their goal of revolution, whilst others insisted on a somewhat puritan approach, refusing to affiliate themselves with any counter-revolutionary or bourgeois movements. This rift in opinion helped to alienate the Bolsheviks from a number of former allies, which, taking the 'puritan' stance, became known loosely as the Communist Left or the 'ultra-leftists',

227

a faction which still plays a role in the contemporary socialist movement.

So, if, in the context of revolution, the debate is still open as to who Marxist organisations should be prepared to side with, how should one go about answering this question? Who should be regarded as allies, and who should be renounced in the struggle for Communism?

One occasion on which this question was brought to light was in 1921, during a period of unrest that occurred in the Communist Party of Italy (PCd'I) following the Comintern's policy of adopting a 'united front', bringing together many workers' movements and associations to strengthen the fight against capitalism. Prominent ultra-leftists in the party, such as Amadeo Bordiga, were greatly opposed to the idea and refused to work with the reactionary Italian Socialist Party, from which the Communists had recently broken away.

Whilst this stance may seem an admirable and dogmatic one, it is important to remember that it is not as though the Bolsheviks (the leading forces in the Comintern) were an opportunist party; they had previously opposed any kind of alliance with reactionary organisations, yet the decision to foster unity between all socialist movements came after a lull in the revolutionary optimism which had swept through Europe following 1917, and a reinstatement of capitalist authority, forcing them to find alternative strategies to weaken capitalism and promote working-class organisation.

The logic of Bordiga and his likes, who eventually lost control of the party to a pro-Moscow group in the PCd'I, prevents this kind of thinking. It asserts that we must form no alliances with counter-revolutionaries no matter what, even if such an alliance would advance the revolution's goals, and thus, through its rejection of such tactical and pragmatic actions, comes into conflict with the essentially Marxist logic of prioritising revolution over any other political goals. This is the reason why it needs stating that 'left Communism' or 'ultra-leftism' does not deserve its leftist connotations; all that divides Lenin and Bordiga is a practical realisation of the revolution's immediate tasks on the part of one, and a pompous, counter-productive ignorance of such on the part of the other. It is no coincidence that Russian Bolshevism, not Italian ultra-leftism, proved victorious in the defeat of the bourgeoisie and the creation of a proletarian dictatorship.

Today, there is an important lesson to be learned from this: one should respect general principles, such as the necessity of distancing oneself from counter-revolutionary people and organisations, but should be ready to break with that principle if it coincides with Communist interests. Obviously, it's unlikely that anyone would cling onto such ideas knowing that they clash with the revolutionary goals; for example, Bordiga undoubtedly rejected Comintern policy with the interests of the proletariat at heart, yet this was a failure to see or acknowledge that the Leninist approach (a pragmatic, logical and ultimately productive manner of thinking) was far superior, and that tactical unity with organisations that may have opposing interests, alongside other sacrifices, may be necessary.

It's worth pointing out that, at the time when the Comintern introduced this policy, only two countries in Europe (Russia and Hungary) had undertaken a successful and independent Communist revolution, and in both cases, examples can be found where such sacrifices were necessarily made. To focus on Hungary in particular, it's a fact that the Communist Party took power by merging with the Social Democrats, after which they established the Hungarian Soviet Republic, set about a programme of radical social reforms and reorganised the economy in a revolutionary manner. If they hadn't partaken in this merger, sacrificing leftist principles for a socialist reality, such change would never have occurred.

> **Yorkafka on November 28, 2015 at 10:29 am said:**
>
> Terrific stuff AR. Prioritising Revolution would (if allied to Utilitarian methodology) require you to ally with anyone who can further the cause. Pragmatism over Purity. There's work to be done!
>
> **chris edwards on November 30, 2015 at 12:15 am said:**
>
> Hi Max,
> How far can one go down this route? If it were thought that short term dalliances with ultra right-wing organisations and/or mass murdering zealots were likely to further the cause of Revolution down the road, would you take the greater good as reason enough to work with such people? History seems to suggest expediency normally wins out.

38. WHAT DO WE MEAN BY 'IMPERIALISM'?

Posted on December 5, 2015

The world 'imperialism' holds a special place in Marxist rhetoric.

Alongside 'revisionist', 'Trotskyist' and various terms denoting bourgeois status, it is a favourite insult of many (particularly Maoists), and has been such ever since it was first theorised by Lenin as the 'Highest Stage of Capitalism'. Yet, whilst popular, it seems that its meaning is not always clear. For example, many socialists would criticise the practices of both Julius Caesar and George W. Bush as 'imperialist', yet their actions were very different, and it's as though this difference is often glossed over.

This can be seen in Mao's Theory of Three Worlds, which groups the USA and the USSR as imperialist countries, Europe, Japan and Canada as 'smaller' imperialist nations, and Asia, Africa and Latin America as the victims of imperialism. Yet the way in which the USA exerts dominance over these parts of the world isn't explained, for, the days of empire now gone, it's clear that such exploitation is predominantly economic only, and perhaps neo-colonialism would be a more accurate description. This is something that I feel is often ignored; when Lenin wrote about imperialism's role in the development of capitalism, he spoke of the British, German and Portuguese empires, yet here, Mao refers largely to the corporate exploitation of the developing world.

Something else left unexplained here is the distinction between western imperialism and that of the Soviet Union, which, unlike the west, did not profit through neo-colonialism. Here, the term refers to the Soviet domination over Eastern Europe or Afghanistan through military and diplomatic, as opposed to economic, control. Thus, though these two forms of domination differ starkly, they are grouped under the same banner.

To clarify the distinction, I believe these two different varieties of imperialism need stating; economic, and military/political imperialism. Often there is overlap, such as in the forceful domination Britain exerted over India for its own economic interests, or perhaps the Second Iraq War, arguably driven by similar interests, yet the differences are clear, despite how often they're ignored.

Yorkafka on December 5, 2015 at 11:54 am said:

While I don't disagree with the thrust of your argument, just a word of warning AR. You write:
  '...the way in which the USA exerts dominance over these parts of the world isn't explained, for, the days of empire now gone, it's clear that such exploitation is predominantly economic only...'
  Caution is needed here, for the US has 780 foreign military bases in more than 70 countries. Russia, UK and France COMBINED have but 32.
  We of course cannot underestimate the global

impact of the golden arches, but there's a lot of military hardware backing it up.

Keep up the good work!

http://www.politico.com/magazine/story/2015/06/us-military-bases-around-the-world-119321

Jacqueline Casey on December 5, 2015 at 1:51 pm said:

I like the subject and I think it is timely given the global situation presently but I think that although the Soviet Union did dominate Eastern Europe diplomatically and militarily this in my opinion did represent a form of neo-colonialism in that the economic output of those dominated countries was pooled into the Soviet pot and contributed to its economic clout. Also the fact that those countries did not benefit from the post-war reconstitution of Europe and were colonised by the Soviet system to my mind deprived Europe of a powerful source of economic energy. Had the Soviets concentrated on their Asian satellites it might have been better for them than trying to hold on to countries that were more natually aligned to Europe.

The leftist lad on December 6, 2015 at 3:29 pm said:

You're so shitting cool.

Anwen on December 11, 2015 at 9:13 pm said:

Hello Max. This is a tad unrelated... Listening to Pick of the Week on Radio 4 last Sunday, I came across a reference to a company called Suma (I checked the spelling on the internet). Founded in 1975, it has a strictly egalitarian pay policy and has existed for 40 years, through a variety of governments in the UK. I wondered if you knew of it...

Nyx on December 22, 2015 at 6:21 am said:

What about Putin's Eurasian Economic 'Union'? Russia stealthily draws its neighbours into an ever tighter economic embrace.

We have all seen how Gazprom is used like a tool... an instrument... I read recently that Armenia's state gas company now renamed Gazprom Armenia. Oh and there's now Gazprom Krygyzstan too (if I've spelt it right). This all looks like economic control to me.

39. HOW LANGUAGE LEGITIMIZES TERRORISM

Posted on December 18, 2015

Following the war in Syria and the rise of Daesh, western society is more determined than ever to curb the number of men, women and children turning to these organisations. Tactics already employed will undoubtedly have some effect; internet censorship will certainly prove useful in the goal of trying to prevent online recruitment, for example. Nonetheless, I believe there's one area where we fall short: the language we use when describing such people.

Surely, if we're trying to lower the number of 'home-grown terrorists' we churn out each year, the last thing we'd want to do is make terrorism sound appealing. Yet synonymous with 'terrorist' are words like 'radical' and 'extremist', which seem to put an exciting spin on the act of systematic murder. After all, when would the 'extreme' ever sound less appealing? When has the 'radical' option never been more attractive, at least superficially? Given that many of the potential recruits we're talking about are children, this likely presents even more of a problem. If it's considered a radical move to join a terrorist organisation, this may help influence such a decision, even if only subconsciously.

Another danger presented by this kind of terminology is the fact that, in the context of Islam, words like 'radicalism', 'extremism' and 'fundamentalism' all imply a sense of untainted purity. They legitimise the doctrine practised by

Daesh or Al-Qaida as a somehow purer interpretation of Islam than that of most normal, law-abiding Muslims, which could present a further danger to the aforementioned crowd. If you cherished and respected your faith, you could easily conclude that an extreme form of that religion – a purer form of that religion – would be favourable. The problem also lies in the fact that this kind of interpretation is wholly untrue; look at most of these organisations and you'll see that they're not really fighting for the caliphate. They're just angry and bloodthirsty people looking for an excuse to kill others.

Now, I'm not suggesting there's a black-and-white separation between Muslims and terrorists, and, as someone very critical of all religion, I'll happily make the point that much of the violence carried out by these so-called fundamentalists is rooted in traditional Islamic principles, yet it seems like they're currently portrayed as more legitimate followers of the same creed. We need to call a spade a spade and accept that sloppy language of this kind only conceals terrorism's ugly reality.

fatherwilliams on December 19, 2015 at 12:17 am said:

Again I find myself wholeheartedly agreeing with you! How hard can it be? And the images, too? Why does Daesh always get to be portrayed parading victoriously in uniform black waving exciting guns?

Helen on December 19, 2015 at 8:11 pm said:

So true! And how hard for our law-abiding ethnic communities! I teach a lot of Muslim students, some of them practising Muslims, some not. Most of them can see through this window-dressing: they are VERY anti Daesh, some quite outspoken. I'm sure they find the present climate pretty uncomfortable.

adrianakent on December 20, 2015 at 1:49 pm said:

Yes, but which words should we use? When young we are all drawn to extremes. We are for or against, lukewarm does not satisfy. Only much later does one think that lukewarm, in an uncertain world, may be the sanest option. If a catholic some girls want to become Brides of Christ… prostrate themselves before the high altar and bid the world farewell. Some enter extreme enclosed orders and may never see family again. Deluded? Yes, but nearly all extreme movements encourage delusions. As T S Eliot has it, Go, go, go, said the bird, humankind cannot bear very much reality. It was not attractive to followers of Hitler, Pol Pot, Idi Amin or any of that ilk – they were just envious cruel megalomaniacs who relished torturing and killing. Fight the good fight indeed…

Charity Norman on December 20, 2015 at 9:42 pm said:

Yes – and I especially agree with your second point about the implication of untainted purity. As for that word extreme – it hadn't occurred to me before, but in modern life it's often used as an accolade. Extreme sports are seen as cool, for the reckless and brave and heroic. Add that to a photo of someone looking faintly mysterious in black, with guns and flags – and the sense that these people have a clan, they have a purpose, they are significant – and your recruitment campaign is underway.

Nyx on December 22, 2015 at 8:26 am said:

Great post. Another brain whirl. The concept of connecting extremism with our innate yet utterly hopeless quest for purity… perfection… our attempts to escape the inescapable (and wonderful) mess that is reality… all partic interesting to think about.

Yorkafka on December 22, 2015 at 6:41 pm said:

But like it or not, these murderers generally profess to carry out their acts pursuant to religious beliefs, albeit perverted religious beliefs. And we have to call them something. Perhaps we should call them 'Perverts'?

Nyx on December 23, 2015 at 7:49 am said:

Yes and agreed, as well as choosing words carefully … we must stop making background images on news etc of IS looking like some sort of badass exciting movie poster… perhaps instead a photo of them pushing a gay man to his death off top of building?

Lucy on December 23, 2015 at 3:18 pm said:

So true. Language is incredibly powerful. I reckon we should create comics showing jihadis as foolish, clumsy brutes – as the Nazis were portrayed in WWII comics – might seem really old fashioned but in fact those comics probably did a good job of helping kids lose their fear of the enemy.

Karen on December 30, 2015 at 7:35 pm said:

Very interesting indeed. I once lived in an area in Belfast where there was a huge mural of a man in a balaclava holding a machine gun. I had to walk past it to go the local shop, given how forgetful I am this was a very regular trip. It began to get to me not because it looked scary or indeed enticing, it started to look normal. I stopped thinking about it or noticing it. Then one of my friends from uni came to visit and kept saying every time she went with me on my many trips to the shop for more milk (ok more wine), how disturbing the image was.

Part of the reason I moved back to England from NI was that I decided that I didn't want to bring children up somewhere where it was normal to have images like this plastered all over the place. I was deeply worried about how it was subconsciously affecting me and my then 2 year old. (You know her, my crazy ginger daughter – might explain a lot.) Whilst I have thought a lot about images and their impact upon our subconscious, I hadn't really thought about the language we used to describe terrorist organisations. I hadn't even thought about the word extremist and its association with the current trend of extreme sports. But then I am an old bird whose idea of extreme sport is running round York in the rain. In Northern Ireland I just called organisations who shot and bombed innocent civilians terrorists – I suppose that was because there were terrorists on both sides. Fundamentalists in my head were different – not involving themselves in the violence but not speaking out against it either. I don't really know why we have changed the language when the terrorists are from the East. Language changes all the time. The word for an Irish rebel which was one held in great esteem – became a word used to abuse a whole religion. Also the word barbarians in Latin meant someone who was foreign (uncivilised) who was not from one of the great empires. It became a derogatory word and then became associated with violence after being described in many of Caesar's works when describing the civilisations he went out to conquer and battled with. I wonder who started referring to terrorists as fundamentalists and extremists, the organisations themselves or us?

One of the major problems I think we face is that we don't know what to call them because we aren't educated enough on who they are, their history, what their motivations are, which are fundamentalist and extremist in the true meaning of the word and which are terrorists. This makes it difficult therefore to label them. I am certainly one of the great unwashed, not really knowing enough to speak on the subject. My husband however purchased a rather interesting book recently called Jihad Academy the Rise of the Islamic State by the French journalist Nicolas Henin (managed first 3 chapters before the Crazy Christmas rush). He was reporting in Syria and got captured and held hostage for quite a while. Luckily he survived and was released. It is for me a real eye opener. I am currently enjoying it, if I ever manage to get all my guests out of my house and return to casual reading will let you know if it's any good.

Anyway as always your blog is incredibly interesting and engaging and forces me every so often to engage my brain.

K

xxx

Andy on January 17, 2016 at 11:28 am said:

Another good and thought-provoking post, Max. Keep going!

I am glad that you call it Daesh, not Islamic State.

The BBC calling the terrorist group Islamic State is another language mistake, as others have pointed out – because most Muslims would not agree it follows the central tenets of Islam, and most other countries do not recognize it as a state.

Calling it this – or similar names like IS, ISIS or ISIL – encourages non-Muslims to see the Daesh killers as following Islam, and conflating Daesh and Islam.

This is dangerous because such confusion leads ignorant non-Muslims to link all Muslims with the idea that some may at least be sympathetic to Daesh, which has consequences for the reception so many Muslim refugees experience arriving in Europe.

I disagree with your view that we should not describe them as extremists.

You are right that we do not want to make terrorism sound appealing. But it is the wrong direction to avoid calling them extremists or radicals: because that is what they are.

As you say, we need to call a spade a spade – and they are extremists, because they have perverted Islam and selectively taken the most blood-thirsty aspects to follow. If we call them anything else, it would be hiding behind euphemisms.

The answer is rather to find other appealing, even extremist, paths for such young and susceptible young men to travel down which are less harmful – football?

If it has to be something religious, there are plenty of paths currently (unjustly) seen as 'extreme' or 'pure' which do not involve chopping off people's heads – for example spirituality.

What do you think?

40. CHRISTMAS UNDER COMMUNISM

Posted on December 25, 2015

Today being December 25th, it feels very inappropriate to write about anything non-Christmas related, and the ideas I've had leading up to this post all seem somewhat out of place at this time of the year. Nonetheless, I believe I've found a way to link the occasion back to the subject of this blog; today I'm asking if Christmas was celebrated in the Communist world.

In the Soviet Union, celebration of the holiday was greatly restricted, and it was suppressed as a manifestation of religion. The League of Militant Atheists, an ideological organisation in the country, fuelled the suppression by promoting an anti-religious and anti-Christmas sentiment, and it is perhaps partly due to their efforts that Christmas is still not widely celebrated in Russia today.

The situation is similar in the People's Republic of China, as the holiday is still not celebrated by many, yet this is less a result of political action than religion; the Chinese Christian population equates to about 1% of the country's 1.4 billion inhabitants, meaning that few recognise the festival's religious significance. This is ever more true in the more remote, western regions, where it is likely seen by many as an alien tradition.

Yet despite this, Christmas has increased in popularity throughout China, and whilst suppressed in the Soviet Union, a separate, secular festival on December 31st was celebrated under the socialist regime. This suggests that, irrespective of whatever religious beliefs they may have, humans want to celebrate something this season. In fact, even the modern holiday we call Christmas wasn't always very Christian; originally a week-long pagan festival concluding on December 25th, it was adopted by Christians to 'draw in' pagan believers, proving that you don't need God as an excuse to celebrate.

With this in mind, I wish everyone a merry, secular Christmas Day.

My decoration of choice

Sophie Weston on December 25, 2015 at 9:38 pm said:

A Friday it may be, but I'm impressed that you've posted a new article on Christmas day, and as interesting as always. A very merry and secular Christmas to you too. I love the red star on your tree...

Yorkafka on December 28, 2015 at 11:24 pm said:

Merry Secular Christmas AR. I'll drink to that.

Karen on December 30, 2015 at 6:48 pm said:

A very merry secular/christian/good excuse to celebrate Christmas to you to. Have a Fab New Year as well. xx

fatherwilliams on January 27, 2016 at 1:11 pm said:

Christmas is actually the only time of year when I go to church, sing hymns, make my children recite them and the Christmas Gospel and try to think about Christianity and its influence on our culture. Why? Because otherwise, i.e. if not a time to remember and consider what our society grew out of as well as enjoy some of the beautiful aspects of Christianity, it is an utterly pointless (capitalistic?) and nauseating consumer orgy. Hallelujah!

41. SHOULD WE SUPPORT INDEPENDENT BUSINESSES IN THE FIGHT AGAINST MONOPOLY CAPITALISM?

Posted on January 1, 2016

The evils of capitalism are often portrayed through huge, transnational corporations, exploiting resources and enslaving workers. Apple, Gap, Samsung and various other brands that have become commonplace in western society are all examples; when people think of the problems capitalism causes, these seem to be the ones that get the blame.

There's good reason for this, as it is these companies that perpetuate injustices so profound that they disgust many across the political spectrum. Largely based in developing countries, they employ labourers to work in appalling conditions for very low salaries, driving the economies of developed nations. Yet, if we're trying to undermine these companies and the economic monopolies they create, is it sensible to turn to small, local businesses instead?

Businessmen of this kind actually occupy a class of their own: the petite bourgeoisie. It comprises people like shopkeepers and local entrepreneurs, and lies sandwiched between the bourgeoisie and proletariat. At first, it might seem sensible to turn to them for the essentials, even if it only means going to an independent cinema, or buying your eggs from local sources now and then. But what if I told you that, by avoiding the corporate giants, by trying to starve them of their consumers, you're only resisting the inevitable?

It is a theory rooted in Marxism that the petite bourgeoisie will eventually vanish, swept up by the bourgeoisie and the proletariat respectively as monopoly capitalism dawns, meaning small businesses will eventually give way to larger ones. We're already seeing this trend occur today, as increasing globalisation allows companies to expand across the globe, and we can sensibly conclude that it will continue to occur until the death of small-scale capitalism. I'm not saying that it's pointless to buy from local sources – it's definitely the morally better option – yet if you're doing it to undermine larger corporations, you're trying to dam a torrent with stones.

Jacqueline Casey on January 2, 2016 at 2:40 pm said:

I really like this piece in that you tackle a subject and a bugbear that opponents of capitalism always pounce on, namely the multinational corporations. I think myself that one reason for buying from local independent traders would be the more personal relationship that they provide in relation to the local community is worth supporting for as long as possible. I agree that I think there is an unstoppable momentum towards full spectrum dominance of corporate power. There is a strange unexpected outworking of this movement however which I think has not occurred to a lot of people and that is the final structure of a fully dominant corporate capitalist system is strangely similar to the structure of a Communist system, the only difference being the purpose and priorities to which the system is directed. The Communist system ideally is providing food, shelter and work for the party members as its main goal whereby the priority of the corporate capitalist system is profit and the members of this system gain access, or not, to food, shelter and work as a side benefit of taking part in this system rather than as a direct result.

Sarah HW on January 2, 2016 at 7:12 pm said:

Hello Max, Sarah here, a colleague of your father, I found this piece personally very apt as I have just been reading Owen Jones' 'The Establishment' (if you don't have this book, I will send you a copy). He argues (and I agree) that the wealthy capitalist elites in the UK could and should contribute far more by way of taxes to society and fund the services we need properly. He outlines how such corporations take from the government constantly (education of workers, their healthcare, housing benefit going to private landlords worth millions, privatisation of NHS etc). At the same time they fund and support a party that demonises and vilifies those who access state benefits. Then you get the likes of Amazon and others exploiting the system to pay no tax while millions of us bear the burden of paying income tax and VAT on our goods. The problem with ending up with a block of corporate elites is that they are in so many ways undermining the very society that makes their trade possible – and we allow them to do this. Late capitalism won't yield a society where people can live well and treat each other well. It makes me want to crowd fund a similar retailer to Amazon and call it 'wepaytax.com'.

Maybe one day…

adrianakent on January 6, 2016 at 10:28 pm said:

Hi Max, but but but… everyone I know buys from Amazon though I don't. What about a list of the companies who do not exploit the workers in developing countries, who pay their full whack of taxes and from whom one can buy with a clear conscience.

adrianakent on January 7, 2016 at 6:31 am said:

P S not buying from Amazon is not virtue on my part: I make no financial transactions on the computer!

42. THE ANONYMOUS REVOLUTIONARY, 2015

Posted on January 8, 2016

This blog, which began last January, is now almost a year old. To mark the end of 2015, WordPress prepared a review of The Anonymous Revolutionary's activities over the past year, and I thought I'd make it public for anyone who's interested.

You may be glad to know a surprising number of people seem to at least sympathise with this website's ideas – a feat I couldn't have foreseen, living in the western world!

Here's an excerpt:

The concert hall at the Sydney Opera House holds 2,700 people. This blog was viewed about 19,000 times in 2015. If it were a concert at Sydney Opera House, it would take about 7 sold-out performances for that many people to see it.